GRACE
AND
COMMON LIFE

DAVID BAILY HARNED

THE UNIVERSITY PRESS OF VIRGINIA

CHARLOTTESVILLE

ISBN: cloth, 0-8139-0379-3; paper, 0-8139-0380-7
Library of Congress Catalog Card Number: 70-171486
Printed in the United States of America

GRACE AND COMMON LIFE

CONTENTS

CONTENTS

For
Christopher, Timothy, and Elaine

PREFACE TO
THE AMERICAN EDITION

Grace and Common Life consists of lectures
given at a center for the study of world religions
in northern India during the autumn of 1970.
In that situation there was little reason for ex-
tensive debate with Protestant theological posi-
tions other than my own, much more for the
exploration of some motif shared by many traditions—grace—and for an interpretation of man—
as player—that is at least not incompatible with
other faiths. In the Hindu scriptures, for example, the universe is regarded as the play *(lila)* of
God, who is, indeed, understood to be ever engaged in play *(nitya lilanurakta)*. In the Sikh tradition, too, grace and playing are prominent
themes. These lectures contain numerous refer-

ences to secularization; the very ambiguous consequences of that process are, increasingly, realities in the Orient as well as in the West.

While skeptical of "natural theology" as an
independent discipline, I am convinced of its significance as an element within the structure of
confessional statements. It is important not only
for purposes of dialogue with those of other traditions, but also so that we might not move too
far from the texture of our ordinary experience—
the pleasures and cares of family life, the games
we play, the changing social processes that shape
and threaten these and, therefore, ourselves.

I want to record several debts. First, to the
National Endowment for the Humanities, for a
fellowship that enabled me to prepare these lectures for publication as well as to pursue further
some of the motifs I touch upon briefly here.
Second, to Miss Charlotte Kohler and the *Virginia Quarterly Review,* for permission to reprint
in altered form some material that first appeared
in the Winter 1971 issue of that periodical under
the title, "The Image of the Player."

DAVID BAILY HARNED

June 1971

INTRODUCTION

This small essay is not an attempt either to map the contours of Christian faith or to defend its truth. Instead, the purpose of these pages is simply to show how this particular faith is born from and nourished by quite ordinary and common experiences which are, in one form or another, perhaps the lot of every man. It would not serve the interests of either piety or scholarship if the differences between Christianity and other traditions were ignored. They are many and they are profound. On the other hand, it would be equally unwise to claim that Christianity rests upon experiences that are less than fully and universally human. Then the stranger might well despair of understanding and the Christian of his own humanity. The attempt to illuminate the relationship between the faith of Christians and some varieties of experience that most men share—whether religious or secular, oriental or western, Christian, Sikh or Hindu— might not only render this one tradition more intelligible to the outsider, but also serve to remind all of us how rich and mysterious is the daily bread of experience upon which everyone feeds.

In the West, man has become whatever he is because of the decisive influence of two factors—the family, and playing with peers. The argument of this essay is that the first furnishes the primary motive for faith in God as well as the fundamental imagery for the expression of that faith, while the latter provides our best understanding of what authentic existence means and affords the most important clue to the nature of the self. Christianity and its future are integrally and, indeed, inseparably bound to the fates of playing and of the family. Perhaps this will seem a rash assertion, especially in the light of contemporary cultural disarray in the West. Robert Ardrey, among many others, recently commented in *The Social Contract* that "what we watch today is the disintegration of the family which we were taught was universal and eternal. It is neither." Speculations equally bleak might be offered about the prospects of play, when so many find surrogates for it in the usage of drugs or the shabby "entertainments" of the mass media, which do nothing to introduce the self to those elements of competition and cooperation, tension and struggle, from which men derive some of their greatest nourishment. But the play impulse is deeply written into the nature of every animal, man not least of all; if his future keeps faith with his past, that impulse will still find avenues for its expression. Whether Ardrey is correct it is far too soon to know. But the interpretation of secularization offered in this essay suggests that while the role of the family will certainly alter, we have no evidence that such change will diminish its importance. We have few certainties, except the knowledge that Christianity has little to hope for if there is no comfortable habitation for families and games in the world of tomorrow.

Some of the dominant motifs of these pages certainly do not represent a consensus among Christians. The emphasis upon the cruciality of the imagination in all human life but especially in the life of faith, the interpretation of the man of faith as above all else a player, the insistence upon the affinities between grace in the households of man and in the household of God, the contention that neither the sacred nor the religious is integrally related to the holy, the reinterpretation of the polarity of nature and grace in the language of play and the everyday, and the stress upon the importance of creativeness—

others, and there are many of them within the
Christian camp, will want to disagree with the
priority awarded to these themes. But few will
quarrel with the claim that grace is a consistent
and critical refrain in the New Testament and
in later Christian thought.

Grace is a theme worth exploration not
only because of its importance in Christian eyes,
but also because of its cruciality for several
other traditions. Perhaps for none of them is it
more central than for the community in which I
am now a guest—the Sikhs. In the interpretation of grace, what we share seems far more
important than where we differ. In *Guru Nanak
and the Sikh Religion*, W. H. McLeod writes of
"the stress which Guru Nanak lays upon what is
normally referred to as divine grace. It is an
aspect which is integral to his total thought and
it is one to which constant reference is made in
his works." Grace is not, however, only the property or preoccupation of men of faith. In the
life of every man there is grace, perhaps not in
any fully theological sense of the word, perhaps
unrecognized or scorned, but still present at
least in the simple gestures and human concern
which grant the newborn a chance for life, a
measure of security, some frail grip upon identity. Grace is there, for the secular as well as
for the religious, as common as the air we

breathe, and as precious. There is little we have that we have not received.

The two parts of this essay conclude with theological arguments. The first is that if the family is as crucial as I contend, then the principal concern of faith is with the holy and the human, not with what is putatively religious or sacred. The second is that if playing is as central as I believe, then the traditional distinction between nature and grace might be much better phrased in terms of play and the everyday. Semantics are not unimportant. The change might render the polarity more intelligible to those who are not Christian and the emphasis upon playing and the player might enable us to recognize the convergence of certain occidental and oriental theological assumptions about the nature of man and his world.

These pages were originally written in conjunction with a seminar on secularization that I taught at the University of Virginia in 1969, then revised for presentation to my colleagues in the Guru Gobind Singh Department of Religious Studies at Punjabi University in 1970. Several pages on the religious and the secular were first written for an international seminar on the teachings of Guru Nanak at Punjabi University in the autumn of 1969, and these were subsequently published in the inaugural issue of the *Journal of Religious Studies*. One of the pleasures that writing affords is opportunity to acknowledge some of one's debts. One of its sorrows is that one can never acknowledge all the debts, for they are many and various. Colleagues and students have a considerable share in the writing of most books, and they do in this.

I would particularly like to mention the Vice-Chancellor of Punjabi University, Sardar Kirpal Singh Narang, who presided over the birth of the Guru Gobind Singh Department of Religious Studies and invited me to join it for a semester. I am proud to own my indebtedness to two friends, Professor Sardar Harbans Singh, chairman of the Department of Religious Studies at Patiala, and Dr. K. L. Seshagiri Rao, my colleague at the University of Virginia as well as University Professor of Comparative Religion at Patiala. Their unfailing patience and graciousness are rare gifts. It is a pleasure to acknowledge what I cannot match. Finally, there are my wife and sons, Christopher and Timothy, who afford the reasons to write and to do all other things. Two boys playing, a family sitting down to eat, a child turning over in the night, a broken arm or a familiar cough—these things are all we know, really, but they suffice.

D. B. H.

Diwali, 1970

PART ONE

FAMILIES

I

GOD: ULTIMACY IN COMPRESENCE

AS Christians understand the matter, *grace* means that man is surprised by a gift he could neither expect nor deserve. It is a gift freely offered; there are no promissory notes to be signed. Even so, gifts unexpected and undeserved foster some sense of indebtedness and gratitude. The man of grace lives *gratefully*, although he is no less autonomous because of that. Quite the contrary; the gift enables him to develop a new attitude and to act in new ways. His range of possibilities grows larger than it was before.

Grace is an insistent refrain in the New Testament, it has sometimes become the dominant motif in Christian reflection, and it has often been employed, perhaps too hastily, to distinguish the Christian from all other interpretations of the relationship between man and ultimate reality. The word describes not only the way that men are brought to Christian commitment but also the gifts that accrue to them in and through Christian commitment. Grace points toward both the character and the consequences of the relationship to ultimate reality that is mediated to man through Jesus of Nazareth and the community that he began. The meaning of the word, then, is what man neither expects nor deserves, nor often wants: God, God with man and for him.

It would be well, however, to qualify the statement that grace means the presence and activity of the divine among men. What is intended by the affirmation that God is personal? Man acknowledges power that is able to strike through to the innermost recesses of selfhood, mystery that is able to grasp and shake the deepest chords of personal being. Such power is liberating, although not in any sense that can easily be deciphered amid the maelstrom of historical events. It is liberating because it unlocks depths of selfhood previously undisclosed, offering new possibilities for man to actualize, new grounds for action hitherto contemplated but never dared. Such power is personal, too, in the sense that its reality is usually

4

disclosed in the context of man's relationships
with other men. But to affirm the presence and
activity of the divine is not to tell of a meeting
between two selves, one human and one divine,
each with its own privacy and independence,
each isolated from other selves. Instead, it is to
see an element of transcendence in what is familiar, cracks in the surfaces of the world like the
ruptures of an icy road in winter. It is to hear
a cry of joy so baseless and utterly at odds with
the evanescence of everything that it burns in
memory like the feel of acid on a hand.

It is true that the New Testament speaks in
a different fashion. The divine is often understood as though it were subordinate to the structure of finite consciousness, to the distinctions
between self and other and between subject and
object. Nevertheless, the contradictory nature
of what the various biblical writers affirm about
God and salvation, church and authentic existence, discloses that the divine cannot be understood satisfactorily in these terms and poses the
problem of interpretation anew for every generation. Herbert Braun has addressed the problem of the lack of harmony in the New Testament and the question of its understanding of
God in this way:

At any rate, God would not be understood
as the one existing for himself, as a species

5

which would only be comprehensible under
this word. God then means much rather the
whence of my being agitated. My being
agitated, however, is determined . . . by being taken care of and by obligation. Being
taken care of and obligation, however, do
not approach me from the universe, but from
another, from my fellow man . . . . I can
speak of God only where I speak of man,
and hence anthropologically. I can speak of
God only where my 'I ought' is counterpointed by 'I may', and hence soteriologi-
cally. For even according to the New Testament, God . . . is where I am placed under
obligation, where I am engaged: engaged in
unconditional 'I may' and 'I ought'. That
would mean then, however, that man as
man, man in relation with his fellow man,
implies God.[1]

Braun comments that what the atheist really
fails to see is man, and concludes that God is a
symbol intended to designate "a definite type of
relationship with one's fellow man". But agency
is an attribute of persons, not of relationships.
Men are not healed or liberated by their relationships, but by the other selves with whom
they come into relation. By analogy, it might
be well for the moment to reserve the name of
God in order to point toward a power at work

6

in man's relationships to himself and to his fellow men, rather than to designate a quality inherent in the relationship itself. Perhaps the relation of divine and human might best be expressed in the language of the *infra lutheranum*: the former is known in, with, and under the latter. Man's transactions with himself and others are eucharists. Grace, then, might be best defined as *the recognition and the reality of ultimacy in compresence.* Such faith is given rather than achieved. It would never be sought had it not been found.

II

HOW GRACE IS KNOWN :
THE FAMILY IN A SECULAR AGE

A gift that exceeds whatever man could expect or deserve—in cognitive terms, then, grace
can be known by grace alone. This claim might
be interpreted to mean that the possibilities of
recognition and acceptance of grace for what it
is are awarded to men only when divine grace
itself is bestowed upon them. But it might more
plausibly be claimed that grace is recognized as
such because intimations and shadows and
rumors of it abound in common life. The primordial form of relationship is the family, a
magic world summoned from chaos by mothers
and fathers. Familial imagery provides a small
but crucial vocabulary that can be "cosmized"
to express faith in ultimate reality. Parents are

8

the first architects of the world, and from their words and deeds one gains the inclination to trust reality, to believe in order—not only within this small and fragile world, but in the great world of which it is a part.

The trustworthiness of being that is implied by the most ordinary maternal actions is more vividly affirmed in times of small crisis. Peter Berger writes of a mother who is awakened by the cry of a child at night. She turns on a lamp, touches the child and sings or speaks. And the content of this communication, Berger continues,

will invariably be the same—'Don't be afraid—everything is all right'. If all goes well, the child will be reassured, his trust in reality recovered, and in this trust he will return to sleep. All this, of course, belongs to the most routine experiences of life and does not depend upon any religious preconceptions. Yet this common scene raises a far from ordinary question, which immediately introduces a religious dimension: *Is the mother lying to the child?* The answer, in the most profound sense, can be 'no' only if there is some truth in the religious interpretation of human existence.[2]

Such assurances are indispensable for the development of selfhood; without some confidence in the trustworthiness of being, the child has

9

neither motivation nor resources to become a man.

The situation of the child, who is loved for himself before and despite his actions, can be described by the phrase *sola gratia* even more aptly than the situation of the orthodox believer. The relationship of parent to child provides images, experiences and assurances that enable one to recognize the meaning, even if not to acknowledge the truth, of Christian claims. These experiences, crucial for the achievement of identity, are instances of grace. The future, to be sure, is in some sense one's own future, and yet its possibilities are shaped by what is given to the self before its own deliberate strivings. Nevertheless, the childhood world summoned by parents from chaos is not safe against the return of chaos. Trust meets betrayal, and private order is violated by the different and conflicting orders and disorders of other worlds. Parental assurances no longer persuade the child that everything is all right. Early experience proves unreliable indeed, as the child learns the father is not divine but finds in this scant reason to search for what is truly ultimate, or then to recognize the divine, when found, as father. The exigencies of the quest for identity counsel rebellion or, at very least, ambivalence toward familial images and roles. So the question asked

10

by Peter Berger recurs. Is the mother lying, unconsciously perhaps, unaware of the implications of what she says? What sort of verification of her words of comfort is typically available, in the experience of passage from childhood to maturity?

Before this question is addressed, however, another demands attention. Perhaps home and temple have been integrally related during much of the history of the West, but is this connection still valid today? In *The Sacred and the Profane*, Mircea Eliade comments extensively on the desacralization of the home. Thresholds are no longer sacred; houses are no longer *microcosmoi* but anonymous, functional, and as disposable as most commodities purchased in a corner store. David Riesman describes a society in transition: *mores* are no longer shaped by the internalized authority of the fathers as much as by the externalized authority of the peer group. Mobility deprives families of any territory that is peculiarly their own, any sacred hearth. The requirements of suburban living constrain fathers to be as notoriously absent as the God whom they were once believed to represent. Most important, the family has lost many and various functions which it performed in earlier versions of society: it is no longer a political or economic or religious unit. These and other changes are

11

often alleged to be instances of the "secularization" of familial life, evidence of the decline of its importance in the modern world.

On the other hand, it seems more plausible to argue, as Talcott Parsons does, that the functions no longer performed by the family were not primarily familial at all. Parsons contends that the family may well be more important in contemporary society than ever before: at least the opportunity is there, because now it has been freed from tasks that are not properly its own. For the first time, perhaps, the energies of the family can be devoted almost entirely to its own fundamental goals, socialization and personal relationships. Recent advances in medical technology, which have dramatically reduced the rate of infant mortality, reinforce the cruciality of the family in an obvious way. Now it is possible for parents to invest in the careers of their children a freight of meaning precluded by the incidence of disease and famine in earlier societies.

Not least among motivations for such investment are certain developments in the public sphere that can properly be described as a process of secularization. What the word really denotes is institutional autonomy, *Eigengesetzlichkeit.* Under the impact of modernization or technological advance, segments of the social structure gain a sort of independence in the twentieth century which they could never claim before: they liberate themselves from a "sacred canopy". In other words, the legitimation of economic or political systems, for example, is no longer derived from appeal to what lies beyond those institutions; they are justified entirely in terms of their own functional logic. They are autonomous. So the individual often discovers, of course, that he can find neither ultimate meaning nor a cohesive set of norms in his public roles and functions. As Thomas Luckmann has phrased the matter:

> Specific segments of an individual's daily conduct derive their meaning from specific institutional norms, but mutually reinforcing institutions no longer endow the individual course of life with "ultimate" significance. The social structure ceases to mediate in a consistent manner between the sacred cosmos and subjective consciousness.[3]

Luckmann warns that secularization can inspire a mass withdrawal into the private sphere while Rome burns. Perhaps he exaggerates this danger. Even so, the impact of technology upon medical affairs and, on the other hand, its contribution toward the achievement of autonomy by the primary public institutions, conspire to add new and deeper significance to the private

13

aspects of life. The process of differentiation that Parsons describes, which liberates the family to perform its own proper role more fully than ever before, suggests that the importance of the family will grow in the future rather than decline. Certainly the increase of time for leisure might also contribute to this. Social change, therefore, does not seem to indicate that the situation of the family will be so violently transformed that the traditional relation between home and temple in the Judeo-Christian world cannot survive. At very least, the evidence is debatable. Both the rapidity and complexity of social change may well challenge the relationship from the other side, however, reinforcing old doubts and raising new ones about the validity of any maternal re-assurance to a child that everything is all right.

III

HOW GRACE IS KNOWN : CRISES, OTHERS, THE UNDISCOVERED SELF

In experience that is common if not universal, the individual finds certain signals or intimations of transcendence. Intimations can be
dismissed; one can discover in oneself neither inclination nor resources for the deciphering of signals; in any event, not all men follow the same
road to Damascus. Still, there are certain typical
experiences—of living with others and toward
death, of crises, and of pursuit of the undis-
covered self—that heighten a sense of the mystery and richness of being, raise anew the question of the trustworthiness of being, and afford
"reasons of the heart" for the cosmization of
images derived from childhood. It may well be
true, however, that the contours and meanings

15

of these typical experiences are blurred, each in a different way, by secularization and allied social processes.

But it is surely true that secularization, because the word connotes a putative loss of agency on the part of the individual in the public realm, can lead to a form of cosmization just as inauthentic and constricting as the one to which religion has often led in less developed societies. The cosmization of familial imagery in response to intimations of the holy is one thing. The cosmization of familial *roles* is an entirely different affair. This is an elemental form of alienation: man identifies himself with his roles until he has lost his freedom, and even the awareness of depths within himself. He becomes nothing but his roles, and the sacralization of these is the guaranty that in his "nothing but" he is properly related to the divine. Because of the ways that secularization can enforce upon the individual a sense of his powerlessness in public and therefore direct him toward the private realm in the quest for ultimate meaning, it tends to heighten the danger of the identification of the self and its possibilities with the familial roles—as daughter, woman, wife, mother and matriarch. Nor is "women's liberation" a sufficient antidote for this. One form of alienation is exchanged for another and the cure is worse than the disease.

16

Peter Berger has defined alienation as "the process whereby the dialectical relationship between the individual and his world is lost to consciousness". Choice, then, bows to necessity, so that

> the individual, who in fact has a choice between different courses of action, posits one of these courses as necessary. The particular case of bad faith that interests us here is the one where the individual, faced with the choice of acting or not acting within a certain role 'program', denies this choice on the basis of his identification with the role in question.[4]

Unless the distinction between the cosmization of familial roles and of familial imagery is maintained, faith rooted in this dimension of experience will inevitably involve a process of alienation and a galloping case of inauthenticity. The sacralizing of roles limits man's sense of the range of his opportunities and responsibilities. The extension of this imagery to all the cosmos, however, renders man responsible in every situation and free as well, for the process of cosmization relativizes the claims of any particular instance of kinship.

The theology of Friedrich Gogarten provides an apt illustration. The revelation of the divine through Jesus Christ means that men who have languished in bondage *to* the world are now offered the opportunity to become responsible *for* it. The Pauline denial that man can earn salvation by his works implies that all worldly activities are radically secular and devoid of religious significance. The same, of course, must be said for all worldly roles, familial or political or economic. All the care and cares of the earth fall within the domain of human reason, and with their desacralization man becomes fully responsible for the world and entirely free within it. Faith, which enables man to move from dependence to autonomy, might best be defined as *Vergeschichtlichung der menschlichen Existenz*—man's understanding of himself becomes fully historical. Gogarten describes the new situation of the believer as one of "mature sonship"—but the noun is decisively qualified by the adjective. The man of faith is mature in the sense that he acts in accordance with his own powers of rational decision, not upon instructions. His sonship is evident in his gratitude for the world that is his patrimony, in his sense of universal kinship, and in his awareness of the mystery of his own origin and delegated independence. The Pauline "denial of works" precludes the cosmization of familial roles, but the cosmization of imagery derived from those roles enables man to acknowledge his unconditional responsibility and freedom, the conjunction of "I ought" and "I may".

There is, then, a dialectical relationship between theology and the familial situation from which it draws its imagery. Theological usage can illuminate the possibilities and redeem the actualities of family life. Experiences acquired during the passage from youth to maturity provide "reasons of the heart" that justify the cosmization of familial imagery. But these experiences also transform the meaning of the images: the latter begin to lose the potential for alienation that they held when they were not yet dissociated from the roles a child plays. Alienation does not involve a fall from innocence: the very young boy or girl knows the self in terms of its roles and has only a small and fragile sense of identity apart from them. In later experience, the focus shifts from dependence to independence, from confidence in the trustworthiness of being to questions about the mystery of being.

In the biography of every individual there are times of crisis, times carefully demarcated from ordinary activity and solemnly celebrated so that they will be fixed in memory forever. Being born and giving birth, choosing a husband or wife and being chosen, choosing a vocation, or a style of life, entering adolescence or a particular community, the days of dying—these are some of the crisis times. It often

19

happens that one is haunted by the sense of an appointment missed. A crisis went unrecognized for what it was. So then memory scouts the terrain of past experience and sets the boundaries of the time of crisis more sharply than rituals could ever do. The mystery and import of the event are reinforced by the difficulty of its recovery. In *Experience and God,* John Smith describes these crises as "times when the purpose of life as such comes into question and when we have the sense that life is being judged, not in its details, but as a whole".[5] Man is filled with a sense of his possibilities—and finitude. These are times of jubilation, but also of dismay.

One reason for the mingling of the two is that in these situations man confronts most vividly the elemental threats to his fulfillment, alienation and anomie, and always discovers that in the past he has been at least partly alienated from himself. The former means that the social order and the roles and functions it offers to the self all confront the individual as inexorable facticities, fates and oppressors. Man believes himself to be, and so becomes, roles and functions and nothing more. The latter means that cosmos is transformed to chaos, that the order in which one trusted has no foundation at all. There is simply no knot in the thread out of which everything is sewn. Death is a paradigm

20

of every time of crisis, for all of them involve a voyage from the landscape of the familiar into *terra incognita.* In every choice of wife or husband, in every decision to have a child or undertake a vocation, there is an element that is arbitrary and absurd. One is ignorant of so many aspects of the person one chooses to marry, of so many exigencies of the vocation one chooses to follow, of so many contingencies involved in the raising of a child. In every critical decision there are these elements of ignorance and arbitrariness. Are they, then, clues to the nature of the world? Do they testify that reality is, in the end, without foundation for its *nomoi* and absurd?

On the other hand, every time of crisis means liberation as well as risk. The self is freed from the constraints of old roles and its range of possibilities increased. In marriage there is a decisive break with the family into which one was "thrown" and a new interpretation of family as a project of the self. The given is supplanted by the chosen. But the roles and functions chosen threaten forms of alienation even more destructive than those a child can experience. Even so, these are still occasions for jubilation, because they disclose something of the bewildering array of possibilities that life affords, something of the depth and mystery of

21

self and world. A birthday party invites a child to celebrate and attend to the mysteriousness of *his* being. Marriage, or a small rite of passage performed in the home, or the birth of a child— these are also reminders that time is not only a continuum in which man is ineluctably driven toward the loss of power and function, but a structure that affords "right times" as well for various expressions of the myriad cadences of life. Existence is too complex an affair to be measured fully by the mechanical patterns of the clock. But there is still reason for an under-current of dismay. The moments when the self is most vividly aware of the richness of its possi-bilities are also the times when the self must choose among them and irrevocably limit what it can become. Among the many selves one might have been, some selves now shall never be. In the curious mixture of fate and freedom which this involves, however, there seems to be an intimation of grace, a clue to the trustworthi-ness of being, that might be clarified by an aes-thetic analogy.

In *Poetics of Music*, Igor Stravinsky writes of the terror he feels at the thought that perhaps everything is permissible. But the seven notes of the scale and its chromatic intervals provide refuge against the threat of anomie and "offer me a field of experience just as vast as the upsetting

22

and dizzy infinitude that had just frightened me". Stravinsky continues:

What delivers me from the anguish into which an unrestricted freedom plunges me is the fact that I am always able to turn immediately to the concrete things that are here in question. I have no use for a theoretic freedom. Let me have something finite, definite . . . My freedom will be so much the greater and more meaningful the more narrowly I limit my field of action . . . . Whatever diminishes constraint diminishes strength."[6]

In the creation of the self, just as in the creation of a bit of music, constraints bring structure and significance to freedom. The legacies of past time and the exigencies of a particular place shape definite possibilities that invest the act of choice with concrete meaning. Fate becomes destiny, in the sense that what is "given" in the self and its situation is what renders the act of choice possible and endows it with significance.

In times of crisis, then, the self may well be aware of an element in its decisions that is arbitrary and absurd, for it is ignorant of so much of the strange and often forbidding territory it must set out to explore. If its decisions provide access to opportunities hitherto unknown or out of reach, they also foreclose forever opportunities

23

the self once could entertain. It is not easy to stifle a sense of anomie, to evade a feeling of the precariousness and finitude of the self, to dismiss questions that seem to have no real answer about the meaning of individual life. On the other hand, one is also conscious of a rhythm written into things that seems benevolent, for it has brought the self to a moment of solemn encounter with itself, to a time for celebration and deep scrutiny, to an occasion for recognition of the depth and mystery and bewildering array of possibilities within both man and world. Man is drawn away from his routines and beneath the surfaces of things. There seems an element of benevolence in reality itself, for the legacies of the past and constraints of the present are liberating as well as limiting. They circumscribe the possibilities of the self but they also invest with determinacy certain options among which the self is free to choose with all proper seriousness, deliberateness and intelligence. In this, there is surely some intimation of grace, even though other types of experience may be necessary before the signal can be read. There is cause to believe in the trustworthiness of being rather than succumb to the sense of anomie. Then, in relationships with other selves, in the discovery of the strangeness of the self that is one's own, and in the anticipation of death, there are other disclosures that support the cosmization of familial imagery and further reduce the threats of alienation and anomie.

There is a difference between experience of others and address by others. In the former, the other is a part of one's world. In the latter, the other *is* the world, for a fugitive moment filling the horizon. Address certainly need not involve speaking; perhaps it need not involve awareness that another is being addressed by or through oneself. The intentness with which the eyes of a child follow the course of a worm through blades of wet grass, or with which an old and solitary woman scrutinizes the surface of her restaurant table, or with which a boy carves initials into cement not yet dry—these may address the self even though the other is quite unaware of one's presence. But touch or word is the apogee of address, when the mystery and exhilaration and fragility of life are counterpointed by the call to responsibility. Hans Urs von Balthasar has commented that

Man must suffocate through man if, in this everlasting meeting with himself which makes up daily life, he meets no one else save man, no matter whether he meets himself in solitude or in community, in solitary community or in the crowds of traffic in the road or on the sports ground. Why should the 'I' lose and offer itself for a 'thou' that, fundamentally, it cannot esteem any more than itself, if nothing else were offered in the 'thou' than that which everyone knows, at least virtually, of himself?[7]

There is much more offered than what everyone knows, however, at least virtually, of himself. Martin Buber contends that the "thou" is always met by grace, never found by seeking, in the sense that the encounter is always unexpected, a surprise. In another sense, there also is an element of grace. The self is transformed, when it is addressed *by* an other, from what it was and is in its experience *of* others. Now it is challenged, and enabled as well, to respond in ways that exceed any capacities present in the routinized world. In Buber's words, "the I of the primary word I-Thou is a different I from that of the primary word I-It."[8] The world in which self is roles and functions is displaced by a new heaven and earth. Times in which the self addresses or is addressed by an other are, surely, neither frequent nor enduring. Nevertheless, such moments are fixed in memory and establish patterns of relationship that survive in the routinized world. They can scarcely be dismissed in the interpretation of human life. In the context of the habits of marriage and friendship, furthermore, another sort of experience can occur that certainly raises questions, and might provide

26

clues, concerning what the world is like.

The face of someone loved seems subtly diffe-rent; it is as though one had never really looked at it before. A wife or son or friend makes a sudden, awkward gesture that invests the whole person with a mantle strange and forbidding. A happy child moans in his sleep and one does not know why. There are times when one is struck by the strangeness and inexorable otherness of a person with whom one has felt a sense of kinship so intimate and profound that it seemed better expressed by touch than words. Neither indiffe-rence nor insensitivity, neither the world that is so much with us nor the passage of the years— nothing can account for the strangeness felt in one who is also so familiar. Yesterday, self and other addressed one another as "thou". Each found through that address a liberation the self could never achieve alone. Memories and re-newals of that intimacy heighten the import of the time today when one confronts a strangeness within the other that will never yield its secrets, a country so remote that no loved one can map all of its terrain.

In this strangeness of one who is familiar there is another intimation of grace, for the expe-rience can act reflexively upon the self, remind-ing one of a richness within the self that trans-cends its powers of comprehension and ability to

27

offer what it is and has to another, even in a
moment of address. The individual is more than
his roles and functions and this more, as it is
glimpsed in the strangeness of another self, seems
bound up with what is most distinctively human
rather than merely animal in man. The self
legitimates its stances and actions in terms of the
roles it plays and the functions it must perform.
Suddenly, however, a man is called to account
or calls himself to account for his acts, without
reference to roles and functions; again, surfaces
are cracked and the mystery of selfhood is discovered anew. There is a perverse instance of
this in *The Fall*, although Jean-Baptiste Clamence, enemy of life and lover of death, manages only to exchange one mode of alienation
for another:

> I had gone up on the Pont des Arts, deserted
> at that hour, to look at the river that could
> hardly be made out now night had come. I
> dominated the island. I felt rising within me
> a vast feeling of power and—I don't know
> how to express it—of completion, which
> cheered my heart. I straightened up and was
> about to light a cigarette, the cigarette of
> satisfaction, when, at that very moment, a
> laugh burst out behind me. Taken by surprise,
> I suddenly wheeled around; there was no one
> there. I stepped to the railing; no barge or

28

> boat. I turned back toward the island and,
> again, heard the laughter behind me, a little
> farther off as if it were going downstream.[9]

The laughter that wells up from within Clamence
and will haunt his future forever reminds him of
an incident a year or two earlier at the Pont
Royal, when he heard the cries of a drowning
girl beneath him but thought no more than,
"Too late, too far . . . ." It was not too late,
then. It is now. The accounts can never be
balanced again. So a man who discovered that
he was unwittingly alienated now chooses a new
form of alienation in a desperate and deliberate
act of inhumanity toward himself.

Consciousness precedes socialization. What is
more, as Peter Berger observes, "it can never be
totally socialized—if nothing else, the ongoing
consciousness of one's own bodily processes
ensures this. Socialization, then, is always partial."[10] Nevertheless, if there are not really vivid
experiences of the otherness of the self and re-
flexive experiences of the strangeness of other
selves, and vice versa, the internal dialogue
between socialized and unsocialized aspects of
the person will lead to little more than indulgent
fantasy. There must be sufficient grasp of the
mystery of selfhood and of the precariousness of
the social world to kindle dialogue into occasional argument, at the very least, if the self is not

29

to yield to alienation, abandoning its freedom
for the security of its roles—and so Clamence.

In these common experiences of crisis and
address by other persons, then, the self discovers
intimations of the benevolence of being, and of
grace and transcendence, that seem to justify the
cosmization of familial imagery. In both types
of experience, there is a strange conjunction of
"I may" and "I ought", a bit of evidence that
the mother of whom Peter Berger writes is not
lying when she reassures her child. In crises, that
into which one has been "thrown" is also that
which invests the freedom of the self with meaning, by spinning a galaxy of possibilities among
which one can choose. In moments of address,
the powers and possibilities of the self are ex-
panded by a reality external to the self. In both,
the discovery of the depths of selfhood, in conjunction with a sharpened awareness of the
threats of anomie and alienation, raises questions about a dimension of depth in reality itself. In both, a sense of the benevolence written
into a situation that liberates and enlarges the
self and the range of its possibilities raises questions about the benevolence of reality as a whole.
In both, a sense of the fragility and ambiguity
of the social world raises questions about whether
there is something more, about how it might be
grasped and best described.

These types of experience, of course, sharpen man's sense of his own mortality. The former, because the choice of certain possibilities means that others now can never be reclaimed. The latter, because it subverts confidence in the permanence and inexorability of the social world. It too is mortal, and man will not inherit everlasting life by way of any role whatever that he plays within it. In "The Death of Ivan Ilych", the dying man reflects that,

> The syllogism he had learned from Kiezewetter's logic: Caius is a man, men are mortal, therefore Caius is mortal, had always seemed to him correct as applied to Caius, but certainly not as applied to himself. That Caius—man in the abstract—was mortal, was perfectly correct, but he was not Caius, not an abstract man, but a creature quite separate from all others. He had been little Vanya, with the toys, a coachman and a nurse . . . . What did Caius know of the smell of that striped leather ball Vanya had been so fond of ?[11]

No time of crisis, except for the imminence of death, freed Ivan Ilych from alienation; always he had hidden himself and hidden from himself among his roles and routines. He had never addressed another as "thou" and perhaps he had never been aware of being addressed. His

31

anguished discovery of his own mortality com-
pelled him to ask, Why? To what purpose?
Whence? But the banality of his experience
and reflections upon experience permits no
affirmation of ultimate meaning.

Ivan Ilych is very much a cautionary figure,
for there is a great deal in contemporary
America that dulls awareness of the finitude of
self and society, blurs the significance of times of
crisis, and dims the sense of being addressed by
other selves. In a fine book, *The American Way of
Death*, Jessica Mitford discusses some of the tech-
niques and rhetoric employed to conceal the
reality of death. Changing social patterns have
conspired to relegate the aged to special colonies
of their own, often very luxurious but still ghet-
toes of a sort. The reduction of the family unit
from three generations to two—as well as the
recent advances of medical technology—has
made death far less a common-place in the household. Within American society as a whole, the
function of what Robert Bellah has called "civil
religion" is not only to legitimate certain
national policies and courses of action, but also
to perpetuate the myth that this one social world
will elude the universal rhythms of growth and
decline. The exploration of the moon is a paradigm of the promise of technology, tempting men
to believe their powers are not limited but limit-

less: while death was once a mystery, now it is no more than a problem that technicians someday will resolve.

Whatever else it might mean, secularization describes an institutional phenomenon that causes men to turn toward the private sphere in their quest for "ultimate" meanings. But even if it denotes something that occurs in the public realm, it can still threaten that search for meaning in the private sector, for the distinction between public and private is really a tenuous and unsatisfactory one. In *The Decline of Wisdom*, Gabriel Marcel writes of the way that reason comes to be identified merely with *functional* reason in an advanced technological society, so that reflection falls into discredit and both the wisdom it offers and the existential questions it raises to the light of consciousness are no longer available to man. Certainly dulled and sometimes buried is the sense of wonder that sparks the awareness of transcendence in man's encounters with himself and others. A notable instance of this is the recent tendency to approach the mystery of sexuality in terms of "performance standards".

So the dismissal of death seems symptomatic of the erosion of significance from each and every time of crisis. The quantification of time in the modern world, as well as the pecul-

iarly American cult of youth, renders it difficult
to discern any sort of benign rhythm imbedded
in human life. The restriction of the range
of reason means that interpretation of times
of crisis becomes increasingly difficult, and
certainly it diminishes the capacities of the
self to address another as "thou" or respond
to another's address. There are some other
elements in the conspiracy, too, although they
may not all be concomitants of secularization.
One is the busyness of life, which seems to have
increased as the basis of the American economy
has shifted from competition to cooperation, as
the disarray of the cities and of their systems of
transport has made commuting more common
and more arduous, and as mobility becomes fact
instead of fancy every year for the one American
family in five that must relocate.

There is also noise—and noise kills. In *The
World of Silence*, Max Picard writes of the noisiness of an age that threatens to reduce man to
no more than "a space for the noise to fill".
What are euphemistically called media of mass
communication invade the privacy of the self
and prevent the encounter of a person with himself that is the prelude to authenticity and
wholeness. The role of the mass media within a
consumer society tends to erode confidence in
words, which seem as meretricious and insignifi-

cant as the products they are employed to vend. The conflict in Vietnam, with its ghastly discrepancy between myth and reality, has enforced upon many the conviction that words cannot really be trusted, at least in their public usage. All sorts of words are preempted and journalized until they seem unable to serve for the interpretation of the deepest dimensions of personal existence. The restriction of the range of reason to functional reason is abetted, then, by recognition that much linguistic usage is "mere rhetoric" and much conversation made only "out of the slimy mud of words, out of the sleet and hail of verbal imprecisions".[12] All these factors contribute to our loss of the sense of rhythm and mortality. But man is mortal and, like all other animals, his life does have a rhythm. Where this is forgotten, man is diminished, the significance of his times of crisis obscured, and illusion becomes a likely candidate to supplant faith.

IV

THE CIRCULARITY OF KNOWING

Many voices, prophetic and otherwise, have expressed opinions about the meanings and consequences of secularization. The opinions have not only outrun where the facts might legitimately carry them, they have probably managed to outnumber the facts themselves. There is very little empirical evidence to support any comprehensive theory about secularization, and considerable evidence that time might be better spent on other sorts of theory. Churches in America proliferate, grow fat and affluent. Astrology and psychical research grasp the popular imagination even more tenaciously than hitherto. Music reminds us everywhere that ours is the age of aquarius. The bourgeois version of the search for ecstasy finds redoutable

36

assistance in drugs. There is no real indication that recent social change either causes or reinforces a "secularization of consciousness" within individuals or communities. It is true, for example, that the contemporary bourgeois child in America is sheltered from the metaphysical terrors of crises and death as his ancestors were not. But he will encounter them nonetheless. There is simply insufficient evidence to determine whether his position of privileged innocence will lead him to respond in "secular" style or will render the experiences so shocking there is no escape from theological reflection. Aspects of contemporary student dissent suggest the latter is as likely as the former.

Nevertheless, there was something of great consequence involved in the debate over secularization. The reality of God is neither an object of immediate experience nor merely an inference from experience. If the divine were immediately experienced, no one would have written very lengthily about "secular man". If the divine were only an inference, a hypothesis offered on the basis of the existence of something else that is manifestly not divine, then secularism would have swept all adversaries from the field generations ago. What is disclosed within the family, in times of crisis, in the experience of living toward death, in moments when one addresses or is addressed by another? The finite is revealed, not the infinite; the human, not the divine—*but the human in relation to the holy,* which is more than can be expected or deserved and all that is necessary. Surfaces are disturbed and one is confronted with a dimension of depth that is one ingredient in human experience. There is no proper sense in which these can be called "religious" experiences. If they seem to justify the cosmization of familial imagery to express faith in God, the grounds they offer, no matter how persuasive, are never coercive. There is no necessity. There is always risk. One who has encountered the depths of existence still need never affirm the reality of God. Why not ?

The answer is that the divine is known only through the interpretation of experience, by imaging and imagining. Unless appropriate imagery is at hand for the organization of experience, the latter will never disclose its deepest secrets. Unless experience has a density and richness tnat will support the imagery by which it is organized, the latter will not long retain the loyalty of the human mind and heart. There is an irreducible circularity involved in knowledge of the divine; unless one begins with God and with images of God, one will never end with him. The process of interpretation enables one to penetrate experience more fully and deeply;

38

the exploration of experience refines and brings new life to the principles and patterns of interpretation, transforming the familial imagery that constitutes man's fundamental resource for the expression of the presence and power of God. John E. Smith properly contends that

All forms of encounter have their appropriate locus, and for the encountering of God we turn to the crucial events of life, to the occasions when the holy becomes manifest. That the crucial events of life represent the disclosure of a concrete, divine reality, however, is not a feature that is to be read off the face of these events. As occasions for the disclosure of the holy, the crises of life remain merely indeterminate until further interpreted through some standard or normative disclosure of God. Such a normative disclosure belongs to the category of revelation; the problem of revelation is a central and inescapable one.[13]

Revelation is a very complex idea, however, not nearly as simple as at first it seems. It designates an experience of crisis, or a moment of encounter with another or with oneself, when a question is raised about the quality or purpose of life as a whole. But experience is not reality but simply a medium in and through which reality is disclosed. So revelation refers to that power which, itself never a single element within experience, grasps and shakes the self. On the other hand, this power could not be acknowledged without the imagery which enables the self to name and address whatever it is that liberates captives, shapes fields of possibilities for the self, elicits questions about authenticity and purpose in individual and social life. These images, too, are an ingredient of revelation. Still another constituent is a community of faith, or plausibility structure, without which acknowledgment of the holy cannot be maintained. The role of the community, even if initially it is simply the family, is twofold. On the one hand, it provides a vocabulary that augments the crucial but meager resources of familial imagery. On the other, its members share a certain interpretation of experience; their convictions are strengthened and maintained by conversations with each other. Experience, power, images, significant others—revelation requires them all.

Because faith involves the interpretation of experience, rather than immediate experience or mere inference or "received opinion", secularization is an important theological issue. But the real questions are not whether man remains *homo religiosus* or has lost his appetite for ecstasy or has attained some sort of allegedly "new" maturity. The problems are three. First, does the

40

contemporary situation in some fashion render it more difficult to recognize times of crisis for what they are and to encounter the depths of the self? Second, have social and cultural change rendered the language and imagery of the Christian tradition far less useful for the interpretation of these critical experiences of the individual? Finally, does secularization consign faith in God to irrelevance within the public domain and, if so, what effect will this have upon faith itself? The movement toward autonomy on the part of primary institutions is accompanied by the further development of institutional specialization in "religion". In other words, because the traditional complex of "ultimate" meanings and norms is no longer disseminated and affirmed by the primary institutions, the main job must be done by a special organization. But when the latter voices many of these meanings, they are exposed as "mere rhetoric". They are not necessarily contradicted by the standards and functional logic of the primary institutions. There is simply no relation between the two at all. Sooner or later, the processes of secularization would seem dramatically to undercut the credibility of the public pronouncements of the churches.

Nevertheless, the famous dictum of Cyprian— "Whoever has not the church for his mother, has not God for his father"—remains as cogent as

ever it was. The world of the individual is con-
structed from a series of conversations. This world
is threatened whenever the really formative conversations are interrupted. But dialogue within
the family is broken by the processes of maturation and by death; times of address by others are
elusive and fleeting. Faith requires a church.
Every faith, even the most secular, requires one.
There must be some structure within which a
certain view of the world is regarded as indisputable and into which new generations are
socialized in such a way that this view is regarded as indisputable by them also. Otherwise, no
continuity to faith. Like man himself, it cannot
exist for long without community. Within this
structure, certain rites or sacraments exist in
order to focus attention upon the critical events
of life, so that the individual may reflect upon
them with proper seriousness. Liturgies and
scriptures exist in order to acquaint persons with
crucial instances of divine presence and with
characteristic modes of divine activity. In other
words, the assumption is that if God is the father
of the Christ, divine activity in the contemporary world will continue to display some sort of
Christic shape. Liturgies and scriptures that represent the way of the Christ are intended to
educate the believer so that he can recognize the
presence and action of God in today's affairs.

These are keys for the deciphering of the significance of the times of crisis that, in their turn, the
sacraments call men to ponder.

The grounds provided by times of address
and crisis for the cosmization of familial imagery
will scarcely prove persuasive if the individual
is not involved in some plausibility structure.
Two of its essential functions are to provide a
new vocabulary and to redeem familial language
from the distortions it has inevitably suffered
because of some aspects of the individual's own
familial experience. Another function, perhaps
most notably accomplished in the Protestant
tradition, is the desacralization of familial roles.
The ceremony of marriage is a paradigm. Two
persons promise themselves to each other, simply
to each other as autonomous human beings, and
neither to certain roles nor to God through those
roles. Marriage involves risk and responsibility;
it is decision, not fate. Similarly, the sacrament
of baptism acknowledges the divine as father
but, equally important, it acknowledges that the
father is not divine. Both he and his child are
liberated from their roles—although, to be sure,
only in certain ways and in relative degrees.
Again, the sacrament of the eucharist furnishes
occasions for parents and children to forgive one
another for their mutual betrayal of their original roles. The former cannot sustain childish

43

expectations of their omnipotence; the latter must throw off the constraints and securities of childhood. The bread and wine are offered for the forgiveness of the betrayal of childish hopes by the human parent, of parental expectations by the maturation of the child, and of the divine parent by both the human parent and the child.

All these rites are intended to achieve the relativization of roles within the family, just as the institution of the sabbath is meant to relativize economic roles and functions, distinctions of caste and clan. They are intended to prevent parents from playing the part of Grand Inquisitor, offering bread and security at the cost of the liberty of self and others—and to prevent children from yielding too much to the blandishments of bread and security, too. Apart from the deconsecration of these roles, the cosmization of the imagery simply pushes the self deeper into alienation. Slavery and slavish dependence find metaphysical justification. The social universe is interpreted in static rather than in dynamic terms, merely as structure and not as process, as a prison from which there is nowhere to appeal for liberation.

But there is another side to the coin. The process of desacralization is not only meant to liberate the self from alienation. Equally important is another function, for it is also in-

44

ended to free the self from the desperate strategy of an anomic choice of negative identity. Erik Erikson has described the phenomenon in this fashion:

> The loss of a sense of identity often is expressed in a scornful and snobbish hostility toward the roles offered as proper and desirable in one's family or immediate community. Any part or aspect of the required role, or all parts, be it masculinity or femininity, nationality or class membership, can become the main focus of the young person's acid disdain . . . . Life and strength seem to exist only where one is not, while decay and danger threaten wherever one happens to be . . . Such vindictive choices of a negative identity represent, of course, a desperate attempt at regaining some mastery in a situation in which the available positive identity elements cancel each other out. The history of such a choice reveals a set of conditions in which it is easier to derive a sense of identity out of a *total* identification with that which one is *least* supposed to be than to struggle for a feeling of reality in acceptable roles which are unattainable with the patient's inner means.[14]

From participation in Christian community, the self is enabled to learn that one need not be perfect to accept one's roles, for these have no sacral

45

status and do not require perfection. The reality
of the divine is sufficient reason to forgive others
who have betrayed their roles, to accept one's
own betrayals, and to maintain one's roles despite various sorts of insecurity. The involution of
desacralization and cosmization provides a way
between alienation and anomie, and the loss of
the sense of the self that both involve.

It is certainly true that Christian community
often fails to serve either God or man. Sacraments lose their reference to experience and no
longer illuminate times of crisis. Liturgies become ends in themselves rather than keys for the
deciphering of contemporary divine action.
Preaching becomes mystification, sacralizing
class *mores* and roles rather than leading to their
deconsecration. Christian vocabulary loses its
cogency for the organization of common experience. So the divine is mislocated, as God becomes a symbol for what putatively lies beyond
the world rather than a symbol for that ultimacy
known in man's compresence with others and
with the earth. The elemental cure for such distortion is the renewal of man's contact with the
density and richness of individual experience.
The actualities of experience can transform and
enrich the imagery and vocabulary with which
one begins the process of interpretation. But the
opposite is also true. One can employ an idiom

that robs experience of its depth and diversity and encourages all sorts ef unwarranted inferences. What principles of interpretation can be developed from, and are appropriate for, explorations of events of crisis and times of encounter with others and the depths of the self? *What is discovered is the holy, and what it is discovered amidst is the human. Their dialectical relationship establishes the primary scheme of interpretation: the holy and the human.*

V

THE HOLY AND THE HUMAN .

Times of encounter with the unsocialized
depths of the self, or with the mysteriously im-
penetrable and irrevocable otherness of persons
whom one had thought to love and know better
than they knew themselves, raise questions
about a transcendent reality within the universe
of which selves form a part. Times of crisis,
when the liberation of the self would be
impossible were it not for the power of
"circumstances" to preclude some possibilities
and render concrete some other options among
which the self is free to choose, raise questions
about the benevolence of reality as a whole.
The questions bite more deeply because of the
imminence of death, reminding the self of
its dependence, of the precariousness of all its

projects, of the necessity for hope and the apparent folly of hoping for too much or for too long. Choice is more momentous because certain possibilities, once rejected, can never be recalled; time sweeps on, and so certain versions of the self, perhaps the best, now will never be. Yet not even the imminence of death resolves in negative terms the question of the benevolence of reality. There are many common joys and pleasures made more intense in the lives of ordinary men simply by the awareness of how ephemeral and fugitive they are.

The life of the family provides the elemental reasons for seeking the divine, and an idiom in which one can address the reality disclosed through all these experiences—a power that seems personal in the sense that it can grasp persons more deeply and intimately than they can grasp themselves. Sometimes the family itself serves as a plausibility structure for the maintenance of faith in God. Even so, sooner or later another structure is necessary. One of the principal responsibilities of Christian community is to serve as a venture in iconoclasm; a crucial aspect of this task is the desacralization of familial roles, so that the cosmization of the imagery of family life will not involve a view of reality as static rather than dynamic, as structure rather than process, or as datum rather than task.

These are the principal claims that have been advanced until now.

What, then, are the consequences of faith in God? Faith means acknowledgment of universal kinship. Nothing is alien to the self, either in the social or in the natural realm. All that is, is valuable, and has its own legitimate claim upon the loyalties of the self, because anything can serve as a medium for the disclosure of the holy. The recognition of universal kinship means the relativization of each and every particular kinship structure. No less important consequences of faith, however, are these two: work is understood as play, and life is interpreted as comedy. The laughter that wells up from within Jean-Baptiste Clamence as he gazes down at the Seine issues merely in what Erikson would call a choice of negative identity. This encounter with the depths of the self is no preface to health and wholeness. Nevertheless, the laugh contains at least a simulacrum of sanity and faith. Julian N. Hartt has written :

> Man does not get on with his proper business in a mood of unrelenting self-seriousness. Contemporary culture lays that mood upon us all. That is a major triumph of secularism as a paradoxically religious force. For if there is no one else to keep an eye on our interests we cannot afford ever to close both eyes or

even to wink promiscuously.[15]

Are there better indices of faith than an occasional promiscuous wink? It is in the primordial form of human community, the family, that one first learns to play. The cosmization of familial imagery means that the whole world becomes an arena for play and that every aspect of the human venture can be understood as a modality of play. If this inhibits the sort of seriousness against which Hartt protests, it certainly does not mean the denial of responsibility. The player is responsible to those with whom he plays and obligated to conform to the idea of fair play; there is seriousness as well as spontaneity in what he does, and the seriousness often increases the enjoyment that play affords. As a voluntary act, play is an affirmation of human freedom. As a social act, it is an affirmation that man is intended for community. As a "useless" act, it is an affirmation that man is more than all his functions and roles—and that he can, indeed, afford "to close both eyes". Man need not, nor can he, any longer judge himself in terms of his works—nor must he yield himself without reservation to the exigencies of his work. Playing means that men turn away from whatever in the everyday world seems "ultimately" serious; they inhabit another realm, one with rules all its own and definite boundaries in time and

space. Whatever else this may suggest, it involves
liberation from the tyranny of the clock and the
quantification of experience. Play is a joyous
affair; it offers many things, but the principal
one is joy. When the whole world has been transformed into the province of play, the benevolence of reality has been grasped well and deeply, indeed.

So faith in God brings joys to man, cannot
help but bring joy, because someone who was
homo religiosus or *homo faber* or whatever is enabled to understand himself as *homo ludens* now.
The "seriousness" of the world is overcome by
the reality of God, and human life discloses itself as a comic business. Comedy has to do with
discrepancy and incongruity. It occupies itself
with the incommensurability between the routinization of things and what is really there to be
tamed and domesticated by routine. It concerns
the shattering of habits and preconceptions and
stereotypes by realities at odds with all expecta-
tion. It laughs at the earnestness with which
men take themselves, at the incongruity between
their postures and poses and, on the other hand,
the ridiculous contingencies and accidents by
which they are continually surprised. The reality
of God, a transcendent criterion of what is
finally serious, means there is some comic potential involved in every instance of seriousness

52

within this world. And authentic humanity comes only by way of the recognition and acceptance of the comic possibilities in all of man's noblest strivings, most altruistic acts, and grandest designs.

More must be said later about play and comedy; their integral relationship to faith in God is adumbrated now only in order to raise questions about some schemes of interpretation that have traditionally been employed in Christian thought. The religious and the sacred seem no more intimately allied with the ideas of play and comedy, and no more directly implied by the cruciality of the family, than are the secular and the profane. The events from which men derive a deeper appreciation of the human and a stronger conviction of the holy cannot properly be called either religious or sacred. So it is difficult to understand why defense of the religious or of the sacred should be associated with commitment to the holy. Religious wiles do not seem sufficient to attain the holy, nor do profane ways seem to bar man from it. In fact, neither is it clear that, as conventionally employed, the distinctions between the religious and the secular and between the sacred and the profane are useful for the analysis of contemporary society.

The polarity of religious and secular is unsatisfactory indeed, because it contributes neither to clarity of vision nor to the increase of faith. Certainly it must not be confused with the distinction between the human and the holy. What is conventionally regarded as "religious" is constantly prey to various types of "secularizing". Religious obligations come to be performed mechanically, by rote, without passion or existential involvement. Motivation for their performance is "secularized" as the obligations themselves are understood in functional terms—not as expressions of devotion but rather done for the sake of gain, sometimes transcendent reward and sometimes mundane benefits such as psychological adjustment. On the institutional level, the religious establishment becomes inextricably involved with the secular in many ways, representing and sacralizing the particular way of life of the people, serving purposes of social control and social integration, reaffirming common *mores* rather than exposing them to the judgment of God. So the "religious", often enough, is not really religious at all.

On the other hand, there is the constant emergence of new forms of religiosity or, if one prefers, of simulacra of religion, within the precincts of the "secular". This is reflected in common linguistic usage: one can be "religious" in one's devotion to sports, to newspaper comics, or to some particular brand of a commodity. While many commentators on the contemporary scene have written about "the secularization of consciousness", it is difficult to understand with what accuracy or by what standards one might gauge the phenomenon—if it exists. Every attempt to measure it risks the danger of some restrictive definition of religion that would quite illegitimately exclude the creation of private structures of meaning which possess "ultimate" significance for individuals who are otherwise alienated from traditional religious symbols and establishments. It would be a mistake, for example, to employ a standard that would not admit the religiosity manifest in the ways in which groups such as family or caste or nation are invested with mythic properties and function as objects of "ultimate" commitment.

The cryptoreligious aspects of the "secular" in contemporary America are legion. There are, for example, a Manichean stance toward life that often appears in political affairs, a Pelagian faith in education as the panacea for all ills, a perennial tendency to celebrate the divinity of power, the sacralizing of the medical profession—these and much else bear witness on allegedly secular soil to a religious impulse as powerful as it seems ineradicable. All the phenomena of psychedelia, the cult of the hero for a day drawn from the realm of entertainment or politics and invested with "instant charisma" by the mass media, the extraordinary efflorescence of interest in astrology and psychical research, the cult of youth with its pervasive cosmetic impulse and faith in drugstore magic, the shamanism of the folk singer, the Gnosticism manifest in certain types of reliance upon drugs, the hardiness of mythologies about sex and all of the *vestigia religionis* imbedded in popular music—all of them suggest the massive presence of religiosity where it is conventionally supposed not to be. A putative secularization of consciousness may pertain to certain traditional systems of symbols, if it pertains to anything at all, but scarcely to the nature of man, whose appetite for ecstasy may be more diffused but certainly seems no duller than hitherto. This state of affairs may very well provide more reason for reflection than for rejoicing. But, if the secular is often really religious while the religious is often secular, what point could there possibly be in the distinction? Certainly the religious must not be identified merely with the ritualized, for the secular has its rites and the most mundane activities, such as the daily round in the bathroom, are often highly ritualized. When "religious" is used in any static and quantifying way, to designate institutions or areas of human life rather than a certain quality of existential participation in these, it has very little meaning. So the attempt to distinguish between the secular and the religious usually leads nowhere except to confusion.

But there are various sorts of confusion, some worse than others. One trouble with this distinction is that, in our contemporary situation, it often tends to involve the juxtaposition of public and private realms and to imply that the latter is good but the former is not. Recent student dissent and black militancy, among other phenomena protesting "the Establishment", suggest that while what Robert Bellah has called "civil religion" may have lost none of its power, at least it is not so widely diffused among all strata of society as it was a decade ago. Then, too, as a description of what seems to be happening to the primary institutions in the public realm, the idea of secularization has real consequences for where man's religiosity will place its bets. The quest for ultimate meaning becomes a private affair in several ways. It is scarcely nourished by participation in the primary public institutions; most must look elsewhere if they are to find satisfactory meaning for their lives. Furthermore, the way that the quest is resolved depends more upon private preference than upon traditional prescription. It is difficult to invest much confidence in traditional religious institutions when their "comprehensive" claims and norms are relevant neither to the functional logic of the primary institutions nor to the performance of the individual within them. In the end, men tend to invest certain aspects of their private lives with a new freight of significance. Religiosity becomes an eclectic affair in which some residual traditional values are combined with others that are new and drawn mainly from the private sphere. The private is sacralized as the public becomes profane.

In this redirection of the quest for ultimate meaning, there is something Manichean about the sharp juxtaposition of two realms, one allegedly sacral and the other profane, which must not be mixed because they have no intrinsic relation to one another. There is something Gnostic about the flight from the constraints of the public sector into the illimitable privacy of the self, in order to "do one's own thing" where illusions of individual autonomy can be savored as shadowy compensation for the loss of real agency in the public sphere. Nor does the constellation of meanings and values drawn from the private realm provide much motivation for greater involvement in the public sector, where individual agency seems to have become problematical in any event. So religiosity is used as justification for the flight from reality and social responsibility. The process of secularization renders religion, ironically enough, even *more* ambiguous a phenomenon than it is in traditional society and reinforces the conviction that commitment to the holy does not constrain men to travel down religious ways. Not only man's encounter with the holy, then, but also the investigation of the actualities of his own common life, suggests the ambiguity of religion and invalidates the distinction between religious and secular.

This emergence of new forms of religiosity from "secular" soil, the retreat from the public to the private for "religious" reasons, the secularizing of what is allegedly religious—these phenomena insistently call for a reassessment of the traditional distinction between the sacred and the profane as well. And the inadequacy of this polarity is disclosed by the simple fact that the sacred can be profaned until it is sacred no longer. Because it can be stained by dirty hands, the sacred cannot very well be essentially related to the holy. As Julian N. Hartt has phrased the matter:

> One might seriously believe that something really holy has in fact been profaned by a religious insistence that it is sacred; and thereafter one might devote great energy and skill to attacking that barrier in the hope that the holy might come into its own. If, that is, one

believed that sexuality were holy one might attack the sacred institutions that have effectively made it dirty and/or trite. And if one believed that freedom were holy one might well feel inspired to attack the sacred institutions that have effectively corrupted it. Thus the sacred emerges as that which men have arbitrarily demarcated as exempt from judgment and change; and thereafter used to protect a stake demonstrably narrower than the common good of mankind. [16]

The sacred, then, is the unstable and arbitrary, a realm within which the exercise of human agency and inventiveness is suspect if not stifled. Distinctions between what is sacred and profane seem always to lead toward idolatry, the confusion of symbols with what they symbolize until the transcendence of the holy over any and all of its manifestations is forgotten. The sacred is presumably intended to point toward an element of ultimacy in human life toward which man might otherwise be indifferent. But the perennial human predicament is not one of indifference toward ultimate meanings but of idolatrous reverence for what is not truly ultimate. The appetite for ecstasy is too imperious to wait for the disclosure of what is genuinely divine. The demarcation of sacred precincts is scarcely a cure for the disease.

60

The same dialectic appears in the relation of sacred and profane that exists in the relation of religious and secular. On the one hand, the sacred is either profaned or eventually becomes a Moloch, just as the religious is vulnerable to secularizing or to declension into magic. On the other hand, what has been profane is frequently sacralized, especially in a revolutionary situation when social change engenders a redirection of the search for ultimate meanings. Sacralization may be initiated as a response to the holy, or it may have lesser and baser motivations. Certain *mores* or institutions may be deliberately designated as sacred for purposes of social integration or control, quite without any concern for the will of God. In any event, the polarity of sacred and profane does not seem to serve the interests of faith in God. Nor is it an apt instrument for cultural analysis. Instead, it blunts man's powers of discrimination, and especially when employed in any static fashion. The distinction is invidious toward the profane and obscures the important truth that profanation can be, and often is, an act of obedience to the dictates of the holy. Man finds fulfillment not in the sacred but only in God.

Modernization and industrialization liberate persons and societies in many and various ways. But it is no less true that one of the salient marks of the modern age would seem to be the loss of freedom and independence by the individual in many aspects of his life, as well as their recovery in certain others. Insistence that one comes to the holy by way of the sacred simply increases the loss of agency and autonomy, exempting still other areas from reconstruction by man's inventiveness. Men's eyes are turned away from public affairs as they search for some putatively sacred realm, or else they accept as functionally sacred what it really lies within their power to change. So the sacred time and again becomes one of the factors that conspire toward the dehumanization of man. Consequently, it discloses itself as the enemy of the holy, for the holy is known precisely in those experiences that liberate selves and require them to exercise their agency. The sacred robs man of liberty.

It is appropriate, then, to protest against the religious and the sacred in the name of whatever is holy and everything that is human. These principles of interpretation cannot legitimately be derived from the typical experiences through which men are grasped by the divine. Nor do they provide resources for further interpretation, except at the cost of severe distortion. Additional devices of interpretation there must be, of course, if faith is to maintain itself, but they are

discovered, quite simply, in a particular community of selves and within the traditions by
which the selves are bound to one another and
to the generations that have gone before them
and will follow after. The resources for the
clarification of experience do not lie in a quite
illegitimate reification called "religion".

In *The Meaning and End of Religion*, Wilfred
Cantwell Smith commented that the meaning
of religion "is notoriously difficult to define". In
some cases of this sort, he continues,

> a repeated failure to agree, to reach any
> satisfying answer or even to make any dis-
> cernible progress towards one, has turned
> out to mean that men have been asking
> a wrong question. In this instance one
> might argue that the sustained inability to
> clarify what the word 'religion' signifies, in
> itself suggests that the term ought to be drop-
> ped; that it is a distorted concept not really
> corresponding to anything definite or distinc-
> tive in the objective world.[17]

Smith argues that the word is inherently ambiguous: it is a generic term, it designates personal piety, it refers to a system of beliefs and
practices available to empirical investigation,
and to the same system understood as an ideal
or essence. More important, the usage indicates
an external and neutral perspective that sees

little of the inner dynamics of faith, for believers
are not concerned with religion but with God.
Finally, the term inhibits recognition of the
historicity of faith and the historicity of the traditions through which faith finds expression.
"Religion" suggests that something dynamic is
really static, that something protean is really
uniform.

The objections are cogent. The experiences
that inspire faith in God are remarkable ones,
but they are fashioned out of the same stuff
from which all man's daily projects and concerns are made. They point beyond the invariably unstable and confusing distinctions between
sacred and profane and between religious and
secular. They point toward the holy. For the
nurture of faith, community and imagery, or
tradition, are necessary. But these cannot be
described as "religion". Christian community
is a human affair, for example, a very earthen
vessel. Many other communities, familial and
political and ethnic, also have their liturgies
and ritual, their hallowed memories and systems
of symbols. All of them attempt to serve man's
incorrigible and often dangerous appetite for
ecstasy—for *ek stasis*, for standing outside himself in union with whatever promises the
redemption of everydayness and defense against
anomie. But if one community is truly different

from the rest, where can the distinction lie, if not in the religious or the sacred?

PART TWO

PLAY

VI

DIMENSIONS OF GRACE

Grace means a gift unexpected and undeserved, God with man and for him. As
Christians understand the matter, grace invariably draws men toward one another. The sense
of the presence of God is ordinarily mediated to
persons by other persons. They speak to us of
God and, by that act, accomplish something
more: for in the experience of their speech, we
come to recognize the reality of the person
hidden behind what we can hear or touch or
see. This primordial instance of the transcendence of the given, this experience so ordinary
and yet sometimes so extraordinary, affords
"reasons of the heart" for attending to the
phenomenon of speech and exploring the
reality behind and beneath the words for clues

to the nature of the self and its world. The initial sense of the presence of God is ordinarily mediated and subsequently reinforced by familial experiences of dependence and trust, love and order, reconciliation and liberation. But the significance of these experiences cannot be fully explored unless the individual appropriates the more expansive and highly articulated imagery of another community of far greater extension, a church. There he discovers that all the language of the Christian tradition calls men from solitude into community, for God is the father of all and the characteristic divine work is the search for the outsider; in Christ there is intended to be neither Jew nor Greek, neither slave nor free. Finally, the maintenance of faith depends upon the continuation of conversations with others who are faithful; commitment cannot survive in solitude. Grace, then, creates and depends upon community among men as well as community between man and the divine.

The Christian church has traditionally been described as a community of acceptance within which the self is empowered. *These are three principal dimensions of grace: community, acceptance and power.* The reality of faith depends upon a significant other who is faithful; the lesson of faith is that the other is significant even if he is faithless; the reward of faith is significance for the faithful and at the same time faithless self that is one's own. Motivation for the acceptance of self and others derives from the gratitude inspired by the disclosure of God. The community acknowledges what renders all of its members equally debtors, possessing nothing of which to boast. They stand together in their common indebtedness. The conviction of experience that one has not found but has been found is strengthened by shared memories of the events on which the community is based. These stories tell of the sovereignty and initiative of a lord who seeks men even when they flee from him, who affirms them even when they are not able to affirm themselves. Because the root of acceptance is gratitude to God, it differs from mere acquiescence to the neighbor, to his aggressiveness and illusions, appetites and frailties. The divine is the source and sustainer of order, the one who liberates man from the tyrannies under which he dwells and which dwell within him. The fact that it is often abrogated and forgotten is no sufficient argument against the old theological distinction between the justification of the sinner and the justification of sin.

Many and various claims, some of them resoundingly excessive, have been made for the gift of power that accrues to men within the church. Perhaps, however, it would be best to understand this dimension of grace as primarily *an enrichment of the imagination.* The possibilities for individual existence at any particular time and place do not significantly exceed—although, of course, they may be much more constricted than—the power of the imagination to grasp what existence is and might become. Imagination has real consequences for ordinary life; indeed, the existence of the human depends upon the survival of a fragile and often threatened store of images of man. On the other hand, images of God and stories of his commerce with man will obviously prove the more efficacious if, in fact, the divine is a reality and is really related to humanity, so that man is not left alone, except for a mighty arsenal of illusions, in his transactions with the world. This enrichment of the imagination, as Christians understand it, shares very little with fantasy, hallucination or dream. Instead, the images insist that the love which is characteristic of God and which Christians are called to imitate is a love of the neighbor, in all his actuality and specificity. They insist that it is in one's transactions with a concrete neighbor that the divine discloses itself. They insist upon the essential historicity of the self, for whom the world and time constitute not a prison but a home. Images of divine activity do not call man beyond history but rather more deeply into all of its density and ambiguity. They do not tell of another world but of the inexhaustible depths and beckoning possibilities of the one we inhabit now.

The self is empowered because it comes to share in a communal past far richer than its own, and finds therein imaginal resources that enrich its perception of the present. This imagery stresses the meaningfulness and potentiality of the future, for it tells of a lord at work in history who promises, "I will do what I will do". Yet it also promises that the future is man's own future, for the images are not so fully articulated that they preclude human creativeness or dismiss the importance of human agency. The self is empowered, then, because it inherits a constellation of myths of separation and return, transgression and penalty and the possibility of reconciliation, conflict and victory, defeat and the transformation of defeat, death and resurrection, with which it can identify and through which it can find clarification of moral vision. Not least important, the person gains an array of very concrete images of the self as moral agent. The conceptual analyis of what responsibility involves has little power to inspire concrete moral action and, more often than not, the exigencies of an actual situation also elude full conceptualization. What is necessary for significant action is an image of the self that will lure the individual to participate in the situation and liberate him to respond in ways that are not dominated by habit and routine.

These gifts of power and contributions to the achievement of identity are strengthened by various rites of passage within the church, as well as rituals for the renewal of acceptance. The former are intended to enforce a sense of rhythm, timeliness and organic development that will complement the meaning of myth and imagery for selfhood, combat the quantification of time that stifles spontaneity and the expression of joy, and awaken the individual to modes of time as various as the worlds within the world. The latter are intended to renew the sense of the worth of oneself and of other selves, and of the worthiness of action in their behalf and in one's own, without which images are impotent and myths no more than dreams. As Christians understand them, these rites of passage and rituals of acceptance are all instances of playing Christ; in a sense, the church is theatre. Identity and acceptance have a Christian significance because they are the consequences of a sort of play that represents the events on which the community is founded. They are genuinely empowering because they are concerned with an enrichment of the imagination that, unlike fantasy, is resolutely focussed upon this world rather than the next, the near rather than the far, the historical instead of the ideal.

Power cannot be identified wholly with the enrichment of imagination, however; so the pursuit of images must be momentarily postponed. First, community means power, in the sense that the self in relation to others gains an amplitude and an expansion of possibilities that it cannot achieve when it is alone. To mention Buber's famous maxim again, the I is a gift of the thou; the realm of persons calls upon depths of the self that the world of things can never liberate. The catholic tradition has called despair the worst of sins, and this might best be described as solitude-in-awareness, the conviction that the human and natural worlds are irremediably indifferent toward the projects and appetites of the individual. Man cannot live without hope, and hope is dependent upon community, upon a system of relationships within which not all possibilities have been exhausted. Second, acceptance means power, in the sense that the self is liberated from absorption with its own anxieties and feelings of guilt. The practice of confession, whether public or private, corporate or individual, releases a significant amount of energy that otherwise would be dissipated in preoccupation with the frailty of the self. Furthermore, acceptance is empowering because it frees the individual from constraints to posture and hide within his roles: the sins are not accepted, the sinner is.

Finally, the community professes complete trust and loyalty toward the One beyond the many, the source and judge of all else. Always there is a disparity between profession and practice, and often there is a quite unholy regard for some community or institution as the normative bearer of the divine. Nevertheless, this profession of faith both legitimates and relativizes all finite claims for trust and loyalty, for God is not only their source but also their judge. Even though it might be no more than an idle dream to suppose that faith is able to reconcile and integrate all these worldly claims, at least it proclaims the transcendence of the self before every demand laid upon it and militates against the surrender of the person to the world of everyday. Not least important, faith in the One beyond the many insists upon the relativity of every claim launched in the name of the church itself, for neither the church nor its imagery must be confused with the divine. Man stands before God

76

as a person, not as a member of any establishment.

But does the interpretation of the church as a community of acceptance within which the self is empowered really serve to distinguish this community from others, whether political or ethnic or familial? The answer is, of course, no, not in any way at all. Every form of human society offers and depends upon a certain hoard of imagery through which a person can understand himself, his relations with others and his situation in the world. Every community involves acceptance and provides rituals for the renewal of acceptance after instances of folly and betrayal. Often, indeed, the actual social functionality of the church adds up to little more than the legitimation of these other images and canons of acceptance in the name of God. The real distinction might be phrased partially, but only partially, in terms of the dialectical understanding the church has of itself as unacceptable before God and yet accepted. The church is called to speak two words against itself: to confess that its members are sinful and that it is a sinful community. Therefore, it can never properly claim to be the normative bearer of the holy. The eschatological imagery implicit within most communities and explicit in Christianity insists upon the radical discontinuity between the church and the structures of man's ultimate fulfillment.

But this sort of institutional humility, even
when it becomes a reality instead of merely a
hope, still does not express any very significant
difference between Christian and other versions
of social organization. Grace means *God*, for man
and with him. In what sense, then, is this really
a community of grace? First, ultimate reality is
disclosed to man within the church just as the
divine reveals itself to men everywhere, especially in times of crisis and encounters with the
depths of the self and of others. But the church is
intended to provide a context of mutual acceptance and direction toward God in which these
experiences are more frequent, or at least more
obtrusive, because of rite and ritual and demarcation from the rush and confusion of ordinary
experience. Furthermore, the presence of God
does not validate itself as such without interpretation. Christians believe that the imaginal resources of their tradition enable them to explore
more deeply and in more discriminating fashion
those instances of divine presence that would
otherwise remain ambiguous and opaque. So
the church provides a context and a vocabulary
for the fuller interpretation of the presence of
God as it is or can be known to all men.

Second, there is the matter of vision not only
more intense but also more expansive. The

stories and memories shared within the community direct the believer toward the world even more often than toward the church. They insist upon the activity of God in the public as well as in the private sphere, in the marketplace as well as in the temple, in world history as well as in the history of a particular community. The consistent orientation of Christian imagery toward the outsider, its emphasis upon God as the "coming one" whose action may be expected everywhere as well as remembered somewhere, its emphasis upon divine work as action to liberate men from bondage to others or to themselves—all these lead to a vision of the divine endeavor that becomes more expansive without the loss of concretion. Still, the crucial distinction does not lie here.

What is most important is that Christian community is intended to be an area in which selves are "radically open" to their own interiority and to that of other selves. Because the person is known by God in his entirety and affirmed despite what remains unacceptable in him, man is liberated for genuine encounter with himself and for the offering of himself to others. Because God is lord, the self is liberated to accept another's total gift of himself without that sense of complete responsibility for the other that is, eventually, too difficult to bear.

Because God is understood not only to call men
to serve their neighbors, but also to disclose
himself primarily in the context of personal
relationships, radical openness provides new
opportunities for knowledge of God and respon-
siveness to him. The usage of "radical" raises
the critical question. Is there some new structure
of existence involved in Christian life, in the
sense in which John Cobb employs that phrase
to designate "what a subject is in and for himself in his givenness to himself"?[1]

In *The Structure of Christian Existence*, he cites
the insistence of Jesus that not only must actions
be loving but motives must be pure, and then
Cobb uses this injunction in order to distinguish
between Christian and all other structures of
existence. Purity of motive, as the biblical
writers understand it, is an "impossible"
demand that cannot be satisfied except by the
presence and power of God. Belief in the holy,
however, and in the cogency of the demand,
does imply a new interpretation of the self.
According to the prophetic tradition in Israel,
the individual man was free to *do* or not to
do what God required of him. For Jesus, the
individual man was free to *be* or not to be
what God wanted him to be. Of course, for
the Pharisee and Jesus alike, what one was
and what one did were inseparable. But

whereas for the Pharisee one was what one did, for Jesus one acted in terms of what one was. The freedom to *be* what one willed to be was a far greater freedom, and hence also a far greater burden, than the freedom to do what one wanted to do.[2]

The freedom and obligation to be what God wants can be fulfilled only "through the Spirit", through the presence and action of the divine within the self. The autonomous individual cannot become what God desires because this involves responsibility not only for what one wills but for the center from which one wills, not only for how feelings are expressed but for the feelings that are never expressed, not only for the motives by which one acts but for a self that acts on such motives. The self is responsible before God for what it is and for what it is not; the nature of man does not provide a context within which he is responsible but, instead, is his responsibility.

This nature is always unfinished, in the sense that every more expansive image of the possibilities and obligations of the self involves an acknowledgment of responsibility for what the self is, and so a recognition that the "I" which acknowledges therefore transcends every vision of itself. Cobb writes:

The essential demand of God has to do precisely with those dimensions of selfhood

which the personal "I" cannot control. To
accept those demands and to accept responsibility to live in terms of them is to accept
radical responsibility for oneself, and that is,
at the same time, to transcend oneself. That
means that the new spiritual "I" is responsible
both for what it is and for what it is not, both
for what lies in its power and for what lies
beyond its power. For the spiritual "I" need
not remain itself but can, instead, always
transcend itself.[3]

There is no justification, of course, for this radical interpretation of man's freedom and accountability except for faith in God. Even so, there
would be no way to act in accordance with it
except for a powerful enrichment of the imagination because, as we have said before, man's
actual possibilities do not exceed his store of
images of himself. So the question of a distinctive structure of Christian existence, one that
involves complete openness toward the self and
other selves and consequently opens new possibilities for commerce with the divine, is best
answered in terms of unfinished man and the
imagination. Man is never finished with his
possibilities for self-transcendence--unless imagination wither and erode the sense of the presence of God, or the absence of God constrict
and eventually destroy the power of imagi-

nation.

What is the consequence of such an interpretation of the nature and potentiality of the human? In the most comprehensive sense imaginable, to use a phrase from Kierkegaard, man is called to, and liberated for, "choosing one's self". To choose oneself means to affirm and accept responsibility for one's own concrete and individual existence. It means to accept responsibility not only for what one thinks and does but for what one is, not only for what one chooses but for the choice of a self that chooses in this fashion. There are no powers any longer and there are no persons anywhere whom the individual can blame for what he is or is not. Choosing oneself means to affirm not only the existence of the individual but also his location at this particular time and in this particular place. Time and place do not constitute fate, for always they are characterized by the possibility of the presence of God.

Choosing one's self is an act of the imagination; the more expansive the imagination, the greater range of possibilities for the self. From man's relationships with himself, other selves and the world, he derives a hoard of images from which his identity is fashioned. The images themselves are often partial, and frequently in conflict. One may demand the repression

83

of certain instincts that have a legitimate claim for attention. Another may blind a man to the worth of certain classes or communities of which he is not a member. A third may enforce some sort of alienation that leads the self habitually to renounce its freedom of choice. The achievement of identity depends upon the reconciliation and integration of these many images. But that process, more often a hope than a reality, occurs only insofar as a master image emerges, one that draws others about itself and transforms them by its domination. Often, however, this master image by which the self grasps itself is not chosen but, instead, is determined by the situation into which the individual is thrown; its hegemony is temporary, soon eclipsed in a different situation that requires a very different understanding of selfhood. So the self is really many selves, not one; it is defined not in terms of its own choices but by the exigencies of the roles into which its various contexts propel it. The person is dissipated away in the world of everyday—its epitaph, fatality of imagination.

What is the master image, then, that is involved when one really "chooses one's self"? What image can dominate in a Christian interpretation of man's nature and possibilities? How can one imagine this new structure of existence? On the one hand, the image must express man's encounter with a reality that is ultimate, the holy. On the other, it must express man's encounter with the human, with himself and others, as radically self-transcendent. Furthermore, it must not involve the sacralization of a particular role, as in the instance of "child of God", for emphasis upon any role whatsoever as a master image threatens the self with alienation. The image here proposed is certainly not exclusive Christian property, although perhaps Christians can find more richly varied meanings in it and greater justification for reliance upon it than some other traditions can. It is the representation of man as *player*. Playing is what life is all about. The image of man as player does not force a particular role upon him but is a protest and safeguard against undue seriousness about any role at all.

VII

PLAYING

Encounter with the holy invests the human situation with a strange mixture of seriousness and unseriousness. It is reason for dancing, for some sort of unbaptized gesture that will snarl the routinized and rationalized world. But there is something dialectical about the dance; it protests against the way the world is only in the name of what it has discovered about the way the world might truly be, against what man has produced only in the name of other passions and possibilities no less truly human. Nor is dancing ever merely a protest; it has its own spontaneity, offers its own immanent and immediate joys. But still, it is no accident that the dance began close by the precincts of the temple, the household of God.

When a man recognizes that he stands in the presence of the holy, life gains a dimension of seriousness that it never possessed hitherto. On the other hand, he is liberated from the sort of seriousness about himself that Julian Hartt regards as one of the principal consequences of secularization. Man is not alone; he need no longer accept the fearful burden of belief that all power resides within his hands. He is free to wink, to close his eyes for a moment, to dance and to dream, to close down the office and go on holiday. If there is God, then man is accountable not only for shards and fragments of his life, not only for the performances his various roles entail, but for himself entire. On the other hand, there is something unserious about this notion of radical accountability. After all, how could anyone be called to account for what he is and for what he is not, for what is possible and for what is not possible for him, for what lies within his control and for what does not? The discrepancy between his responsibility for himself and his power over himself surely has more than enough comic aspects. Furthermore, while the divine acts to liberate man and to persuade him to wrestle with the exigencies of this new freedom, at the same time the reality of God means that man must finally be unserious about whatever opportunities and duties are

87

afforded by the powers and principalities of this world. Then, too, the crucial locus of divine activity is the imagination, which seems in the eyes of the everyday world the least serious of human powers, for it has so little apparent concern with the "ordering of priorities", with what is prudent or feasible.

Playing can be profoundly serious, so at first there seems to be no intrinsic relation between the play impulse and comedy. Nevertheless, the interpretation of self as player is most congruent with the twofold discovery that the universe has suddenly turned comic and yet, within it, man is called to more radical responsibility than he could hitherto imagine. The image captures the mixture of liberty and limits that authentic existence involves; it affords necessary resources for traveling the narrow way between anomie and alienation, the loss of all the gods or surrender to gods which are less than holy. Most important, it is only when playing affords the master image of what it means to be a man that one is fully freed to "choose oneself". In other words, play is the strongest possible affirmation of the self apart from its roles and functions and everydayness. Then, too, this affirmation occurs in the context of conflict or tension; not all play is an attempt to win a victory, but usually

there is some some stage at which the outcome of the game is in doubt: there must be
struggle, inventiveness, the use of human agency.
Playing is also a paradigm of imaginative activity : one must imagine that time ends with the
ninth inning or that space concludes with the
hundredth yard. The more complex its form,
the more profound its vindication of imagination
as the distinctive ingredient of selfhood. And it
is imagination that will ceaselessly furnish new
visions of the meaning of selfhood, providing
new options that lure men to move on from
familiar territory, to choose more, and to choose
again. To choose oneself involves the acceptance
of discipline, order, limitation. But in understanding the self as player these are not encountered as "fate". They are accepted for the sake
of the game, freely chosen because there is no
constraint to play this particular game. The self
grasps and affirms a certain constellation of
limits precisely for the sake of its own creative
fulfillment: choice displaces necessity.

In his classic study of the phenomenon,
Johan Huizinga describes play as, first of all, a
voluntary activity. One never needs to play
except "to the extent that the enjoyment of it
makes a need".[4] It expresses a sort of elemental
freedom and agency and, just for that reason,
becomes all the more important as seculariza-

tion and allied processes offer men grounds for
doubt whether they remain agents or dwindle
to patients in many and various aspects of life.
Second, according to Huizinga, "play is not 'ordinary' or 'real' life. It is rather a stepping out
of 'real' life into a temporary sphere of activity
with a disposition all of its own."[5] For a moment, at least, it insists that the "real" is illu-
sory and the "illusion" is real. Consequently,
the image of the player manages to express the
discrepancy between man's apparent situation
and his address by a power that transcends the
world. He is a player, nothing more—and nothing less. But this description of life does not detract from either its seriousness or its moral dimension. Play *is* serious and can absorb the self
utterly. It involves rules and limits; it depends
upon a certain order and this, indeed, is its
third essential characteristic. It has limits in
time and space, and those who enter its precincts accept those limits and bind themselves
to a code, a set of "rules". Playing is nomizing:
it transforms a chaos into a world.

Despite all that initially seems to distinguish
play from ordinary forms of human activity,
Huizinga argues that "the great archetypal
activities of human society are all permeated
with play from the start."[6] Even in their most
sophisticated forms, they still betray their

origin. The urge to play is the force that sustains and refines our technology, our philosophy, our diplomacy and jurisprudence :

> Even those activities which aim at the satisfaction of vital needs—hunting, for instance—tend, in archaic society, to take on the play-form. Social life is endowed with suprabiological forms, in the shape of play, which enhance its value...By this we do not mean that play turns into culture, rather that in its earliest phases culture has the play character, that it proceeds in the shape and the mood of play. In the twin union of play and culture, play is primary.[7]

Men always need to be reminded of the inextricable entangling of civilization and the play impulse. Recognition of what inspires and sustains even the greatest of human achievements is perhaps the most salutary cure for the temptation to invest with ultimate significance standards that are provisional, styles that are no more than ephemeral and evanescent, tasks that are really games. It seems the best antidote against man's penchant for measuring himself and others in terms of functions, roles and services. Acknowledgment of the play impulse certainly has firm theological warrant: the disclosure of what is authentically divine renders all else unserious by comparison. But there is a different side to the matter, as well.

The interpenetration of play and culture raises the question of the role that play performs in the socialization of the individual. Playing has no end beyond itself; its appeal is profoundly related to its useless and gratuitous character. Even so, the institution of the family and the satisfaction of the play impulse have been the two primary instruments of socialization in the history of the West. Playing not only offers man release from the pressures of vital needs, it ushers him from isolation into community. It brings people to a common place, enforces upon them common rules, gives them a common aim. It teaches respect for form and limits, instills a sense of fairness, heightens and refines the competitive impulse and our creative instincts. Play is the school in which children learn to understand a discipline or code not as arbitrary and external authority but as intrinsic to the continuance of the game, indispensable for the satisfaction and development of the self that playing can afford. It is by way of playing that persons learn the importance and the requirements of life together with their peers, and in this fashion are children prepared for the adult world. And the interpretation of the latter as a complex of forms of play affirms the importance of human agency and imagination, of struggle and inventiveness, and of fairness as a regulative principle in every enterprise of man.

The element of play that penetrates each aspect of the human venture, as well as the function of playing in the socialization of the individual, would seem to justify the image of man as player in two different senses. It expresses the self as given and as chosen, as animal and as human, as instinct and as freedom; it captures what the self is and what the self is called to become, nature and history. The two primary instruments of socialization within the Judeo-Christian tradition, then, afford the imaginal resources for the Judeo-Christian understanding of both God and man: the divine is grasped through the cosmization of familial imagery, the human through the master image of the player. But more must be said of the implications of the latter for interpretations of the world and of time, of the self and of the loss of the self.

Few expressions of the play impulse are as pure as the venture of the artist; painting and poetry, for example, give expression to the sort of dialectical affirmation and negation of the world that playing always involves. In *The Rebel*, Albert Camus writes:

Art is the activity that exalts and denies

93

simultaneously. 'No artist tolerates reality,' says Nietzsche. That is true, but no artist can get along without reality. Artistic creation is a demand for unity and a rejection of the world. But it rejects the world on account of what it lacks and in the name of what it sometimes is.[8]

In the form of every painting there is some sort of implicit protest, although sometimes so muted it can scarcely be heard, for reality is "humanized", reorganized to afford greater visual pleasure. Then, too, the emotion that art expresses often discloses man's ambivalence toward the world. Nevertheless, the referend of aesthetic activity remains the world in which we live, no other one, and the creative venture celebrates the stuff of which this world is made. Indeed, the exigencies of the materials with which the artist works have their own significant role in the determination of what he will create. In every form of play there is the same dialectic of affirmation and negation, sometimes stated and sometimes merely implied. It is implicit, surely, in the way that certain varieties of play establish a private realm, an inviolable time and space within which there is an order never more than roughly sketched within the great world outside.

The dialectic is equally evident in the stance

toward time that playing involves. In some games, the passage of a few minutes is critically important. But it is not enough to say that play has temporal limits: the clock can be stopped, and often it is. Time quantified reigns, but its reign is provisional and subject to interruption. In still other forms of play a whole new structure of temporality appears, time measured in accordance with the rhythms of the human heart, and *kronos* is banished for the duration of the game. Man is freed from his bondage to the sort of quantification of time that robs life of rhythm, but freed by and for another modality of time more deeply human. Again, and especially within the arts, imaginings of what the future might be can be expressed without regard for any ordinary canons of feasibility. Yet these intimations can exert powerful suasion upon conscience in the present and widen the range of actual possibilities. Never becomes not yet and quantified time yields to a portentous invasion of the present by the future.

This dialectical stance toward the world and time which is at least implicit in every form of play has, for the Christian, considerable theological significance. It is always congruent with, and can become a very clear expression of, response to the transcendent power that sustains and judges man, God the liberator and lord.

95

The power to stop the hands of the clock even when the game is played by the rules of time quantified, to move from the latter into a different modality of time, to grasp the future imaginatively so that it becomes a real power judging the present and inaugurating a new galaxy of present possibilities—these are congruent with, and can well and clearly express, the Christian apprehension of God as "the coming one", the lord whose every advent is a *kairos*. Not least important, the dialectic of play is the elemental form of human ecstasy—one stands a bit outside the everyday self and its world. A taste for ecstasy can be a dangerous thing, but in any event the appetite for more than the factual order is too imperious to be denied. At its best, play advertises that the exigencies of authentic selfhood transcend the routine claims of the world, and it judges them partial and provisional by the same movement through which new possibilities are grasped that can redeem the times. What better way to satisfy the thirst for ecstasy on this side of the kingdom of God? "I can plot a course," writes Julian Hartt,

> that will carry me out of the agonies and blandishments of the factual order of things into a vastly richer world of make-believe. I can convert all or the gist of life into a game;

and confess that the rules thereof are set by
a mysterious Player to whom the game belongs even though he may not appear in it
in his own form . . . . Enjoying the form and
power of the Game I may reasonably
suppose that the factual order at its very best
is only a part of it and quite the least significant part at that. The transcendent Player
did that with his left hand. Why then should
I treat the System with the deadly seriousness it ordains?[9]

Among all the images of man that compete
for our allegiance, that of the player seems most
inclusive of the human commonwealth, most
expansive in its grasp of the individual self,
most important for the growth of community.
While much has been written of the need to recover the dionysian element in life, the vein of
imagery such literature has mined is thoroughly
irrelevant to the problems of the aged and the
dying, the weak or guilty or, not least of all,
those who make the decisions in a manipula-
tive and exploitative society. But as playing can
enable the young to explore the future, so can
playing enable the aged to recapture the past;
the terrain of memory is as rich as that of anticipation. No one is excluded from play by the
loss of power or function. Nor is the appearance
of death unchanged when viewed from the pers-

97

pective of play. Death is not disguised or evaded; instead, it is recognized as simply the end of the game. Like every form of play, life also has its limits in time and space; absorbing and serious though it is, life is played out within some vaster structure of which the player remains unaware until the game is done.

The impulse to reconcile Dionysius and Apollo, vitality and order, can be realized only by an image that portrays order as intrinsic to the expression of vitality. It is useless to call for the recovery of the dionysian or of the apollonian unless there is some image of man that can present these principles as not merely juxtaposed to one another but internally and integrally related. The player is someone who chooses order for the sake of expression of the joy, power and spontaneity that could not find significant release apart from this nomizing activity. While the image of the player implies the provisionality of all finite structures, tasks, and ways of perceiving, it certainly does not erode confidence in structure and struggle as such. The interdependence of order and vitality, especially in the play of the artist, is expressed by Igor Stravinsky, who has frequently written of his dizziness before the abyss of liberty without constraint. Potentiality bereft of structure or determination is a wasteland, and breeds "a sort of terror when, at the moment of setting to work and finding myself before the infinitude of possibilities that present themselves, I have the feeling that everything is permissible to me." He speaks of the importance of structure and constraint, contending that for the artist "whatever diminishes constraint diminishes strength."[10]

Alienation waits for anyone who follows Apollo too closely: the self is lost in society. Man regards his roles as fate; he forgets that he is a co-producer of his world and loses any sort of spontaneity or creativeness. The player, however, is a participant and, at least potentially, never merely a spectator; the image underscores the role of the individual as a co-producer and not simply a victim of the social order. Especially when the disorders of society enforce upon the individual grave doubts about his agency, the image is crucial. The possibilities of existence may be less rich than one's images of selfhood, but they can scarcely be greater. After all, one has nothing else to go on. At least the figure of the player offers grounds for the attempt to act in decisive and innovative ways within the public realm. On the other hand, the danger that awaits the apostle of Dionysius is the loss of community, for community cannot survive without a structure: the self is lost in nature.

The player is conscious of distinctions between yours and mine, theirs and ours. But the other is not an alien or an outsider, and therefore never really an enemy, for he is a defender of the same order and a participant in the same game. Even the venture of the artist has its role in the maintenance of community. A painting or novel is a vindication of the powers of the self to create and share meanings. As an intelligible act of expression, art testifies to the possibility and asserts the importance of communication among men, and so it is a statement of faith in the value of community. Art never says I alone, but always you and I, for otherwise there would be no reason to offer one's vision to someone else.

The player is most inclusive in its portrayal of the individual self because it stresses both order and vitality, intention and spontaneity, the social and the private dimensions of selfhood. The image emphasizes the social aspect of the self not least of all simply because of its focus upon the imagination. At bottom, the lack of love is nothing more than a failure of imagination. From whatever perspective one looks at man, this power emerges as the principal architect of selfhood. It is by imagination that *homo sapiens* grasps the material about which he will reason; it is by images that *homo faber* is empowered to act and build for himself a world. It is imagination that enables man to live in the future. The privilege and burden of such life is what distinguishes him from all else on the earth, and is often the way by which he comes to acknowledge the reality of God. On the other hand, the idea of play invariably implies the creation of some "private" realm, some more or less inviolable time and space that bears testimony to the transcendence of the self over its roles and functions and place within the world of everyday. Perhaps this is one of the most significant aspects of the image within a society that has become increasingly skeptical of the notion of privacy and increasingly unwilling or unable to offer it to the individual. There is privacy to the imagination of the player, privacy not all the mass media will manage wholly to violate.

The image of the player, then, stresses the importance of order, but it never speaks of order for its own sake; structure is important only because of its integral relationship to the expression of all the wildness and wilderness of human passion and vitality. Sometimes the world threatens to return to chaos, but imagination can still re-enact and renew the mystery of creation. It can spin out a thousand new worlds powerful enough to ingest the individual and involve him in some new *nomos*—and so, for example, one identifies oneself with a character in a novel or with a community that extends in time and space far beyond the reach of the individual. However bleak the prospects of the everyday, however threatening the visage it turns toward the individual, a man can still construct a bit of time and space with its own logic, its own demand for fairness toward both others and the self.

The creation of private spheres in which human liberty and spontaneity are at home testifies to man's irrepressible thirst for ecstasy, to the limitations of the factual order, and to the partiality of functional norms and utilitarian patterns of thought. The distinction between player and spectator emphasizes man's role as a co-producer of every world in which he stands: no world nor any role within it is encountered as "fate" and nothing more. This sense of the individual as co-producer, the loss of which is the principal meaning of alienation, is reinforced by the character of play itself. Commenting on the higher forms of play as either contests for something, or representations of something, or else a combination of the two, Huizinga writes of the element of tension that all playing involves:

Tension means uncertainty, chanciness; a

striving to decide the issue and so end
it. The player wants something to 'go',
to 'come off'; he wants to 'succeed' by his
own exertions. Baby reaching for a toy,
pussy patting a bobbin, a little girl playing
ball—all want to achieve something difficult,
to succeed, to end a tension. Play is 'tense',
as we say . . . . Though play as such is outside the range of good and bad, the element
of tension imparts to it a certain ethical
value in so far as it means a testing of the
player's prowess: his courage, tenacity, resources."[11]

Finally, to see oneself as a player lessens the
threats to the identity of the individual that are
posed by radical change and times of crisis.
The contemporary world is, indeed, the scene
of very great social changes. The image of the
player can prove a significant antidote against
all the new possibilities for bad faith that
appear when familial and personal relationships
are invested with a greater freight of meaning
than they can properly bear—as putative compensation for what happens in the public
sphere.

Playing is a biological instinct. But to grasp
the self as a player, and so in the fullest sense to
choose oneself, is much more than the expression
of instinct. Where this master image is embrac-

103

ed because one has encountered the presence of the holy, man is a *grateful* player. Gratitude will find some way to show itself. What is most appropriate for the man of faith? How should he play in the presence of God? *The ultimate expression of gratitude is creativeness, for which God has offered to man the room and the resources. Herein lies a fourth dimension of grace, one that depends upon community and acceptance and employs the enrichment of imagination that power denotes.* Man is intended, in a very precise sense, for *creative play.*

VIII

CREATING

To write of creativeness is not to initiate a
new theme, for the motif is implicit in much of
what has already been expressed. The player is
someone who builds worlds that have their own
special time and order and frontiers; their power
to ingest the player himself is the force that
holds at bay the threats of anomie, alienation
and the tyranny of the everyday. The greatest
significance of the image, however, lies in the
resources it provides for "choosing one's self".
In other words, man is enabled to understand
his selfhood as his own project rather than his
fate: the self becomes its own creator. To speak
of creation only with reference to the produc-
tion of some artifact reflects a singularly constricted point of view. The most profound and

105

important expressions of creativeness have to do with persons, not with things. The making of a novel or poem is simply a more disciplined extension of the creative linguistic usage by which all men organize and interpret the worlds in which they live and the worlds that live within themselves.

The means by which man is armed for choosing the self is the imagination, the source of every form of creativeness. It is the imagination that creates a future and endows it with sufficient determinacy to lure man onward toward tomorrow. It is by way of images that man is enabled to function in the present. It is the imagination that presents ever new visions of selfhood, so that man cannot rest content with what he was yesterday but must engage again in the creative venture of becoming fully human. The holy is recognized primarily when old certainties dissolve and the self must strike out into *terra incognita*, when one discovers again mysterious depths within the self that warn against surrender to old roles and constraints and the alienation they involve. *The holy appears, then, precisely when the self cannot take refuge in what is familiar but must accept responsibility for itself, must choose and create what it will be. There is an intimate correlation between the disclosure of the divine and the acknowledgment that*

106

man must create himself. It is *he* who must live. He cannot be lived by others. He cannot live through others. But the autonomy to which man is called is a gift as well as a demand, so there is cause for gratitude toward the mystery of its origin and end. Finally, the holy is known as the depth hidden beneath the surfaces of life, the really real, the supremely actual. Its appearance, the liberation it offers, the gratitude it breeds—these call man above all else to create new actualizations, to realize powers and possibilities so that the realm of the actual will be greater and richer than it was before.

The theme of creativeness is a sort of ground bass that unites the different melodies of the master image of the player, the act of choosing one's self that the image serves, the role of imagination in the achievement of selfhood, the times of disclosure and functions of the holy in human life. Within the Christian tradition, just as the principal means for the expression of faith and trust in God have lain in the cosmization of familial imagery, so also has it been the family that has provided the elemental sphere for the expression of creativeness. Far more important than the mystery of birth or the rudimentary socialization of the child, creative ventures though these are, is the hazardous affair of the liberation of an adolescent to be what he or she wills to be. The sacrament of baptism serves to remind Christians that, in the end, every child belongs to God and is not meant to be possessed by its parents. Consequently, while no one can avoid raising his children more or less in accordance with his own standards and values, the proper goal of that process cannot be construed as the acceptance by the child of those particular canons. The latter are important, finally, only because of their contributions to the openness and discrimination with which the child will explore for himself the values the world holds, and to the faithfulness he will display toward whatever he finds deserving of loyalty and love. In the whole realm of human relationships, little is more creative, or more profoundly analogous to the work of the holy, than the preparation and liberation of the child to be what it wills to be. The father who wishes too much to see himself in his son does not gain a sort of immortality but, in robbing his child of its own independent futurity, has abbreviated his own life as well. Instead of creation there is only repetition, and repetition is always gratuitous.

Nevertheless, as Dostoyevski's Grand Inquisitor understood so poignantly, it is easier to offer bread than liberty and most difficult of all to offer liberty to someone whom one loves. The act is always shadowed by imagination's grasp of how vulnerable the human is to ways of the world that are random, abusive and coarse. On the other hand, as the Grand Inquisitor also knew, it is easier to accept bread than liberty. Freedom is threatening, for it demands the exercise of powers yet untested, ventures into territories still unknown, separation from those with whom one has most closely identified and sought to imitate. The process of maturation breeds inevitable uncertainties and anxieties as old patterns of familial relationships are disturbed and transformed. Consequently, the family is the primary area within which the need for reconciliation arises; it is also the primary area within which the motivation for reconciliation exists, for it is a structure created by love and mutual dependence. *In the realm of human relationships, reconciliation is the highest form of creativeness and most fully discloses what creativeness involves.*

Love can see beauty and dignity in a face that reveals nothing remarkable to casual scrutiny; love can uncover and unlock a whole array of possibilities within both lover and loved one, of which they may not hitherto have been at all aware. But, in the end, love can breach only the walls that persons are ready to surrender. The act of reconciliation can breach even the walls that persons are ready to defend. Reconciliation means the reunion of the separated, each of whom was divested of individual possibilities, as well as of the possibilities of their relationship, by their estrangement. The renewed relationship is much more than the restoration of the *status quo ante;* old options are restored, indeed, but genuinely new possibilities have also emerged because the relationship has gained an additional dimension through its reaffirmation. Love can actualize possibilities that lovelessness cannot even discern. But it is the gesture of reconciliation that can restore what has become a wasteland from which all potentiality was temporarily excised, as well as most greatly enlarge the domain of the possible beyond what it had been hitherto. So the man of faith is intended to be an agent of reconciliation. As the work that contributes most to the expansion and actualization of human possibilities, reconciliation is also at the center of the works of God. The supremely actual cares supremely for the enrichment of actuality. The cosmization of familial imagery implies faith that God is the supreme reconciler and presents the whole world to man as a sphere in which he is called to emulate this divine work.

In *Cry, The Beloved Country,* Alan Paton has told the story of a man who searches for his prodigal son. The father is a black country priest, Stephen Kumalo, whose quest ends in defeat and humiliation, for he discovers that his sister is a prostitute, his brother a charlatan, his son a murderer. The murdered man is named Arthur Jarvis and his father is a farmer whose lands surround Stephen Kumalo's village. In the course of the novel, old Mr. Jarvis emerges as a sort of prodigal son who is sought and found by the divine father. The original familial image is invested with new dimensions and presents the world as the arena of the reconciling work of God. At the funeral for his son,

> People that he did not know shook hands with him, some speaking their sympathy in brief conventional phrases, some speaking simply of his son. The black people—yes, the black people also—it was the first time he had ever shaken hands with black people.[12]

There are intimations of providence in the fear that grasps the land, as recompense for its pervasive betrayal of moral possibility. As Arthur Jarvis wrote of those for whom reconciliation was not the goal:

> We shall live from day to day, and put more locks on the doors, and get a fine fierce dog when the fine fierce bitch next door has pups, and hold on to our handbags more tenaciously; and the beauty of the trees by

111

night, and the raptures of lovers under the stars, these things we shall forego . . . . We shall be careful.[13]

On the other hand, there are also intimations of providence in the development of a strategy of reconciliation that opens new and richer possibilities than existed before. A night of terror, in which a boy murdered a man whose name he did not even know for a few dollars and some whiskey, has strange fruit: out of it have come a dam for an arid valley, an agronomist to work for the renewal of some dessicated farmland, milk for some undernourished children, a good many brothers for someone who lost a son, love for a land that before had been raped, some breaches in the hardness of the human heart. The Biblical imagery of fathers human and divine in search of their prodigal children portrays the reconciliation of man with man as the most creative of human acts precisely because of the divine activity that is its constant support and context.

But it is never easy to recognize this context for man's creativeness, for divine activity, to state the obvious again, does not validate itself as such. One must find principles of interpretation and discrimination if the world is to disclose its labyrinthine ways. On the other hand, the cosmization of familial imagery seems never more than a very dubious venture, not only because of the actual ambiguities of human experience but also because the family so often becomes a structure of destruction within which reconciliation is notable only for its absence. Parents offer bread instead of freedom or else permissiveness is interpreted as lack of love. As changing social processes often conspire to invest the family with greater significance than the institution can bear, there arises a sort of familism in which selfhood is identified with one's role as mother or father. The American ideal of "cooperation" and our contemporary veneration of youth seem to constrain parents to try to be "liked" by their children above all else, at all times and in all places and at no matter how high a cost—to be accepted, in some sense, not as elders but as peers. So the fulfillment of the traditional role of authority figure depends upon how fully one succeeds in attaining the status of peer! The irony is as exquisite as the consequences are destructive for parent and child alike. Satisfactory performance tends to be gauged for everyone in terms of how well one is liked. Instead of reconciliation, which acknowledges the violation of order, there can be nothing except confusion or surrender in this orderless situation. Encounter with the holy judges and transforms the familial situation,

113

however. It emphasizes the integrity of the self beyond its various functions and relations, but also the legitimacy and importance of the latter, and so it establishes that idea of *order* which reconciliation must presuppose.

Some varieties of play are more creative of authentic selfhood than others, while still other kinds contribute nothing to selfhood at all because they are not true instances of play but merely simulacra of it. In other words, some of its crucial ingredients are missing: perhaps order or spontaneity, perhaps privacy or the disruption of chronology, or else celebration or inutility or struggle. Some forms of ecstasy, of standing outside the humdrum self by participation in a greater power or community, lead to the loss of the self. Others heighten all the powers of selfhood far beyond their ordinary actualization in the routinized world. In *Man for Himself*, Erich Fromm contrasts productive and nonproductive types of human character; the distinction illuminates some of the difference between authentic and inauthentic forms of play.

The reigning nonproductive stance among contemporary citizens is what Fromm calls the marketing orientation: man experiences himself as a commodity whose value does not depend upon what he can do as much as upon how he can *seem*. Success becomes a function of persona-

114

lity; what matters is not whether one is useful
but whether one is fashionable. So a man's
sense of his own worth finally comes to depend
upon factors beyond his control—the vicissitudes
of public taste. Fromm comments upon the insecurity that is inevitably fostered by this orientation. One's sense of worth and selfhood depend
principally upon the approval of others, and the
only way such approval can be gauged is in
terms of status, success and prestige. So one
looks away from oneself instead of toward oneself. Man no longer has any real experience of
his own identity: it consists merely of the images
of him that others hold.

The mature and productive individual derives his feeling of identity from the experience of himself as the agent who is one
with his powers; this feeling of self can be
briefly expressed as meaning "*I am what I
do.*" In the marketing orientation man encounters his own powers as commodities alienated from him. He is not one with them
but they are masked from him because what
matters is not his self-realization in the process of using them but his success in the process of selling them. Both his powers and
what they create become estranged, something different from himself, something for
others to judge and to use; thus his feeling of

115

identity becomes as shaky as his self-esteem; it is constituted by the sum total of roles one can play: *"I am as you desire me."*[14] Whether or not a man trapped by the marketing orientation understands himself within it as a player is really immaterial for, after all, no significant self is affirmed or liberated by that recognition. Even though one understands the game for what it is, each new investment in it diminishes the likelihood of choosing one's self. The elements of authentic play are not there—transcendence, striving, liberty, privacy and the rest. What is needed, of course, is not an understanding of the self as a player of roles *within* the situation, but an image of self as player that will enable it to *transcend* the situation, and establish itself anew.

In his discussion of productive man, Fromm is careful to distinguish between productivity and activity. In his often frantic round of activism, contemporary man finds few occasions for reflection about the ends for which he acts. Ends become simply means toward further ends which can never be specified, and so the whole world is effectually instrumentalized. Activity is not experienced as evidence of one's own agency and autonomy; it is inspired by the need to gain the approval of others and shaped by the relentless pressures of the everyday. Consequently, man

116

seeks "power over" because he has been deprived of "power to": domination becomes a surrogate for capacity. "Power over" is the perversion of "power to", Fromm writes:

Where potency is lacking, man's relatedness to the world is perverted into a desire to dominate, to exert power over others as though they were things. Domination is coupled with death; potency with life. Domination springs from impotance and in turn reinforces it, for if an individual can force somebody else to serve him, his own need to be productive is increasingly paralyzed.[15]

Genuine productivity is a matter of contemplation as much as action; in a world where so much is frenzied and too rapid, precipitate and sudden, little is more creative than the act of imaginative contemplation that enables man to encounter himself and penetrate more deeply into the mystery of his commerce with the world. The elemental motivation for such creative ventures as art and literature is simply that man might *see* more, see more expansively and profoundly into the ways of the world and of the human heart.

Fromm prefers the idea of productiveness to that of creativity, however, because the latter seems to imply the making of an artifact. "While it is true that man's productiveness can

117

create material things, works of art, and systems of thought, *by far the most important object of productiveness is man himself*."[16] It would be difficult to quarrel with the contention that humanity is the true goal of creativeness, but Fromm concerns himself with the capacities of the individual to such an extent that he cannot recognize the importance of reconciliation, and of the sacrifice of the self, in creating new and richer possibilities for human life. His unremitting focus upon the autonomy of the individual does not allow him to pay sufficient attention to the importance of order and authority, or to acknowledge the truth of Stravinsky's observation that whatever diminishes constraint diminishes strength. From a Christian perspective, however, still more important is the difference between the assertion of the productive man, "I am what I do", and the claim that "I am a player". When Fromm contends that, in effect, to *do* is to be valuable, what concerns him most of all is the distinction between the autonomous expression of one's own powers, or on the other hand, the experience of one's capacities as alienated from oneself.

But the figure of the player, even though it emphasizes vitality and competition and agency, very strongly suggests that to *be* is to be valuable. The first and elemental testimony that playing affords is that man is more than the factual order can recognize. The principle of valuation is not the expression of one's capacities but the citadel of selfhood that underlies every expression, not agency or operation but being itself. Real play is always celebration of life and of living and what life might someday be. A member of a family is not loved because of what he can be or do but simply because he is *there*; in the same way, in experiences of the depths of the self and of other selves, the holy is associated with the richness and unfathomable mystery of being. Both the situation from which imagery is drawn for the expression of faith and the experiences which undergird faith imply the claim that to be is to be valuable. As Christians understand the matter, this is supremely expressed by the New Testament story of the love of the cross, which accepts and affirms all that is even in the moment of exercising judgment upon its distortion.

There is another fundamental implicate of times of crisis or encounters with the interiority of the self. Christians have traditionally opposed synergism, the belief that man and God are mutually active in the achievement of man's salvation, for this has seemed to detract from the majesty and power of the divine. But in synergism there is real truth: in his encounters with

119

the holy, man is liberated to accomplish what God himself cannot do. No father can be a man for his son, no mother a woman for her daughter. The holy can liberate a man to choose and actualize what he will be, but the holy cannot live that existence for the individual. So man has a role to play with God in contributing to the realm of the actual; without man, reality would remain forever poorer, bereft of the actualizations that only the terminal finite individual can achieve. Salvation means health, wholeness, complete actuality; that actualization depends upon man no less than man depends upon the supremely actual, God.

In *The Destiny of Man*, Nicolas Berdyaev discriminates among the ethics of law, of redemption, and of creativeness. His argument is somewhat flawed by a tendency to separate as well as distinguish the three: little is said, for example, of the authority of law even within the life of the believer, of the creative significance of reconciliation, of the cruciality of order or "law" for the expression of creativity. Nevertheless, the distinctions are vital ones for, out of the reach of his freedom, man is meant to continue the work of creation.

Man is not a slave, still less a mere nothing, and he cooperates with the divine task of achieving a creative victory over nothingness. Man is necessary to God, and God suffers when man fails to be conscious of his own usefulness. God helps man, but man must also help God.[17]

The liberating work of God and the creative vocation of man are refrains that inform everything Berdyaev wrote, and for this reason alone he remains one of the most seminal Christian minds of the century. The importance of creativity lies above all in its affirmation of whatever is unique and individual, the actualities that have never been before and which could not ever be except for the agency of this or that particular person. Creativeness is resolutely opposed to "they say" or "one does", to the humdrum and repetitive. It is concerned with what has never been, with the not yet, with the might be—and so it is man's best defense against idolatrous reverence for the powers and principalities of the present. It exalts the imaginative over the normative. It reminds apollonian man that life is process and that "moral life must be determined not by a purpose or a norm but by imagery and the exercise of creative activity."[18] Finally, it sees in the ambiguities of time opportunity as well as cause for anxiety; the future holds *kairoi* for creativeness to fulfill as well as the dangers of frailty, accident and age. Life is oriented toward the

121

future, not the past, although not even the past
is ever past for the creative man.

Creativeness has to do, finally, with persons,
not with things. The aim of the enrichment of
imagination that the Christian tradition can
provide is liberation for the creative act of
choosing one's self. The myths and imagery
offered to the individual are intended to enable
him to participate in the contemporary work of
God, the liberation of the captives, the *creatio
continuata*. Through both the images and the
events from which they arise there runs the constant theme of reconciliation, beckoning men to
participate with God in this paradigm of the
creative act. What, then, does creativeness really mean? Who can tell, if it be genuinely creative? We must wait and see. The reconciliation
of the separated, the liberation of children and
captives, the preparation of persons to exercise
their freedom with passion and discrimination,
a garden or a drawing or a gesture of affection,
a bit of whistling or the sense of the presence of
God. Sometimes it is content with the evanescent, sometimes it is in search of permanence.
But always, at least indirectly, it contributes to
the enrichment and formalization of the realm
of the actual. Creativeness has many meanings,
and the discovery of some of them must wait
upon whatever is done tomorrow by God, un-

finished man, and the power of imagination.

While Berdyaev wrote of man's participation with the divine in the creation of new meaning and value, Karl Barth emphasizes a different aspect of the matter which is equally important for the interpretation of grace. He cites Luther's "amazement" at the goodness of God the creator, who "does not will to be alone, but to have a reality beside himself". And, Barth comments:

> Creation is grace . . . God does not grudge the existence of the reality distinct from himself; He does not grudge it its own reality, nature and freedom . . . Is it not true that if we confront existence, not least our own existence, we can but in astonishment state the truth and reality of the fact that I *may exist*, the world may exist, although it is a reality distinct from God, although the world including man and therefore myself is not God?[19]

The lines capture the sense of liberation and indebtedness that the resolution of certain times of crisis evokes—although one may not even know to whom or to what one is indebted. But they also suggest that, although the primary meaning of grace is that God is with and for man, the word has a second, but by no means secondary, signification.

Because a man has encountered what is veritably holy at certain times and places, he is forced to acknowledge the absence of the holy from other places and times. Precisely because he *has* been grasped by the presence of God, however, he cannot now interpret divine absence to mean indifference, as though he had been left alone in a wasteland and was the prey of its random tyrannies. The holy enables a man to choose himself. The holy does not live the existence of the individual, however, as we have said before, but allows him a realm for the free expanse of human liberty. God does not grudge man his own finite life, but is known most intimately when recognized as the one power that unfailingly affirms the independent existence of the terminal finite individual and awards him time and room for play. The presence of the holy is indispensable for the fulfillment of the quest for authentic selfhood. But the absence of God is equally necessary for the fulfillment of that quest. Both are instances of grace. *One of the most distinctive aspects of the Christian tradition, therefore, is that the idea of grace designates both the presence and the absence of God.*

So there is real and unavoidable tension between two ways of phrasing the meaning of Christian life; both are valid and neither must be allowed to obscure or exclude the other. On the one hand, creativeness is a participatory affair, cooperation in the reconciling work of God by someone who has schooled himself to recognize the traces of contemporary divine activity. In *Bread and Wine*, Ignazio Silone tells the story of an aged man whose son has been tortured and killed during a police interrogation. Among those who visit old Murica are some who were enemies of his son, others who are strangers. Nevertheless, he transforms the common courtesies of a host into a eucharistic act. Now there is seed beneath the snow and eyes that will recognize it when spring returns.

Old Murica, standing at the head of the table, offered bread and wine to the men around him. He poured out the wine and said, "Drink," and broke the bread and said, "Eat!"

"It was he who helped me to prune, spray, weed, gather the grapes of which this wine was made. Take and drink this, his wine."

Beggars arrived.

"Let them come in," his mother said.

"They may have been sent to spy," someone murmured.

"Let them come in."

Many, giving food and drink to beggars, have fed Jesus without knowing it.

125

"Eat and drink," the father said. "This is his bread and this is his wine."[20]

On the other hand, creativeness can equally well be an act of independence, a gesture of autonomy, oriented toward nothing except the existence of some artifact. In the same way, there develop two contrasting moralities, one concerned primarily with redeeming the times and contributing to the work of God, and the other with building new and imaginary worlds for the delight of human sensibility, one oriented first of all toward the holy and the other toward the expression of the capacities and possibilities of the self. So, in a sense, the man of sanctity and the secular man may have equal title to be called Christian, especially when the imagery by which men learn to recognize the contemporary presence of God is oriented so strongly toward the *saeculum*, calling men forth from the temple as well as toward it.

IX

GRACE IN NATURE

New opportunities for socialization, various possibilities for acceptance, different forms of empowering—these are gifts offered to any and all men whenever they commit themselves to other persons or powers or institutions. They are granted to the individual simply because he is "thrown" into certain familial and cultural and national groups. All such relationships afford resources for the organization of experience, the achievement of identity, the development of the social self. Certainly it must be recognized that some of these can encourage the alienation of the self and others can foster partial and vicious interpretations of life. Even so, it is formally true that the triadic experience of community, acceptance and power is not something esoteric, known only by a privileged few. It is a fact of ordinary life, acknowledged in various ways by all men, no matter whether they are "secular" or "religious". In this sense, grace is not the antithesis of nature but lies within it, is the secret that lies at its heart, awarding distinctively human identity to organisms that otherwise could never achieve it for themselves. Grace is inescapable: without it, the animal cannot become a man. Furthermore, as James Gustafson has carefully argued in *Treasure in Earthen Vessels,* the ways that grace is mediated in and through the Christian tradition do not differ formally from the ways that it is mediated in and through the structures and conversations within other religious or "secular" communities. It is precisely the analogy between natural and Christian experiences of grace, as this is recognized in the cosmization of familial imagery, that renders Christian language meaningful and therefore makes Christian commitment a significant option.

The traditional Christian theological polarity of nature and grace must be approached by way of the common experience of grace in nature. From this perspective, however, the conventional polarities of sacred and profane and of religious and secular seem even more anomalous. Grace is first discovered in the realm of the putatively secular and profane, not in the precincts of the sacred. Emphasis upon the similar roles of various sorts of community as vessels of grace underscores, first of all, the fact that as Christians understand the matter grace, even at its most magisterial and eminently theological, still is *humanizing*. It does not remove one from the human lot but renders one's lot human. Grace may well be understood to "crown" nature, as the tradition phrases it, but only when this affirmation is interpreted in historical rather than metaphysical terms. In other words, only by way of the experience of community and acceptance and empowering can the natural organism achieve any specifically human identity. What is mediated to the individual through churches is important only because it can counterbalance as well as augment other resources for the fulfillment of selfhood.

Second, attention to the parallel can serve to rectify some traditional and mistaken attempts to distinguish sharply between nature and grace, or common and saving grace, or prevenient grace and human freedom. The venerable catholic distinction between "common" and "saving" grace was an attempt to give some theological honor to those elements in ordinary life which provide individuals with a sufficient sense of security to relate themselves to others and express the love of others. Unfortunately, however, this vocabulary has tended to separate the two forms of grace rather than unify them, and it has masked the actual ambiguity of "saving" grace as well. Reinhold Niebuhr has wisely remarked that the latter, according to theory,

> is induced by a religious experience in which the conscience of the individual self transfers devotion from a contingent community, such as family, race or nation, to an ultimate loyalty to God, the fountainhead of the whole realm of value. Actually the force of "saving grace" has a different course in history than the one marked out for it according to the theory. It has emphasized the loyalty of individuals to the immediate community, rather than emancipating them from idolatrous worship of common loyalties.[21]

Niebuhr also argues that the distinction is invidious because of the way that it tends to exalt "individual experience above social experience and thus obscures the social factors which redeem the individual from undue self-concern."[22] It is a difficult road from childhood to maturity, if not an impossible one, unless grace prevenes in the form of familial security, the expression of love and devotion by

parents which will inspire what Erik Erikson
has called "basic trust". The situation of child
in family can be characterized by the phrase
sola gratia as well as, if not better than, the
situation of believer in church. The difficulty
with this watchword of the classical reformation
is not touched by the traditional catholic objections to it; the real problem is that the reformers
never adequately explored the foundations in
ordinary experience for their claim, "so little
do we have that we have not received". The
sacrament of infant baptism is an expressive
paradigm of that grace written into our common life without which Christian claims would
seem to make no sense at all. A third reason
to insist upon the importance of this parallel is
implied in the last of Niebuhr's comments. Just
as all other social forces and structures are
ambiguous and can become structures of destruction, so can the church. And it does. The
notion of grace can cloak some weird combina-
tions of ultimate commitment and parochial
loyalty. What is cited as grace can very often
be no more than a simulacrum of the genuine
article. In the church, then, as in the society
of which it is a part, there is always the interpenetration of authentic forms and corrupt
simulacra of community, acceptance and power.

Nevertheless, Christians believe that the deci-

sive instance of grace in this world is bound up
with the presence of God for and with man in
Jesus Christ, and in the community that bears
his name. But what is meant by "decisive",
especially in the light of the actual ambiguity
of every church? On the one hand, every social
structure mediates grace and various simulacra
of it to the individual. On the other, the transcendent power toward which the Christ points
is the ultimate source and ground of all that
is. So the theological resources derived from
Christian faith first of all demand recognition
of the *continuities* between all these various
instances of grace. Revelation in Christ, therefore, is "decisive" not in the sense that it is
isolated from or unrelated to natural social
processes, but precisely because it enables the
individual to envision the latter and the self in
the light of their ultimate source and end. The
decisive instance of grace is simply the one that
allows man to interpret himself and his world
with the greatest depth and discrimination and
coherence. The greater the understanding of
existence, the more riches it holds.

What are some of the consequences intended
to be when one relates himself and his experiences of grace to the name of Jesus, the Christ?
First, it is primarily the family that provides a
child with the security and basic trust which

enable an individual to love and to offer himself to others. But no social structure, whether family or caste or nation, can escape sufficiently from its own communal self-interest for the unqualified pursuit of the welfare of other families or castes or nations. The cosmization of familial imagery means that parochial loyalties can be relativized and, even more important, that the faithful self limitlessly extends the realm within which he will act on the assumption of basic trust, and therefore increase his possibilities for fulfillment. Second, and certainly no less important than the extension of the realm that supports basic trust, there is that new understanding of the self which is concretely expressed by the image of the player and which complements what John Cobb calls a "new structure of existence". Man is made responsible not only for the motives on which he acts but for the self that acts on such motives. But this sense of radical responsibility is liberating rather than oppressive, because now one is free to "choose one's self" in accordance with the master image of the player—and gain the autonomy it involves, the defenses against anomie and alienation it provides, the reconciliation of Apollo and Dionysius it promises. Third, to relate oneself to the name of Christ is to recognize that

man is called to creativeness and that the idea
of grace designates the *absence* as well as the
presence of God. The absence of God and of
the gods is grace, certainly, in the sense that
it permits man to strive for his own maturity
and furnishes the necessary room for the free
expanse of his capacities. He is awarded what
is at least intended to be a wholly secular
realm.

If this family or nation is sacred, then either
other families and nations are not sacred or else
whatever violates familial and national interests
generally conceived is not sacred. If one thing
is sacred, presumably something else must be
secular or profane. If one recognizes something
as profane, it might even be argued, one has
been grasped by the sacred. But the argument
of this essay has been that it is the polarity of
the holy and the human which is of importance
for theology, and that the holy is not integrally
bound up with anything else at all except for the
authentically human. Therefore, it is possible
to argue that the consequences of the partial
desacralization of the world that follows from
faith in the gods of nature and history are very
different, indeed, from the results of the far
greater desacralization of things that follows
from faith in the one God beyond these contingent deities.

From a theological perspective, "secularization" can have three meanings. First, it can suggest that the quest for the holy is abandoned, that men no longer thirst for the sort of *ek stasis* in which all the powers of the self are driven beyond their actualization in the routinized world. But there is no persuasive evidence whatever for this understanding of our contemporary situation. Quite the contrary seems true, in large part because of our increasing affluence. Second, secularization can designate the condition of the remainder of the world, after the holy has been identified with a particular sacred power or community. This is the consequence of any variety of faith in the gods of nature and history. Third, the word can also imply that the quest for the holy has become diffused beyond the normal precincts of the sacred or the religious. The dominance of functional norms and the development of institutional autonomy in the public realm and, on the other hand, the proliferation of private forms of religiosity, testify that this sort of secularization is a pervasive phenomenon in the modern West. It holds great and various dangers for the Christian tradition. In another sense, however, it is quite consonant with that tradition and largely inspired by it: for Christian faith, as we have said, there is no integral relation between the sacred

135

and the holy and intimations of the latter are discovered precisely in the most ordinary and recurrent of experiences. Recent claims that Christian faith is synonymous with secularity have been rash, to say the least, but in the precise sense of the diffusion of the quest for ecstasy beyond the realm of the conventionally sacred or religious, secularization is a proper and important product of Christianity.

The consequences of the second and third types of secularization are very different. In the former situation, men of faith tend to be indifferent, exploitative, or hostile toward whatever lies outside the realm of the sacred; all that is greatly valuable is equated with what is sacred. In the latter, all that is, is valuable. All experiences are possible media for the disclosure of the holy. In the former, the opportunities for the expression of collective egotism have few bounds, for the putatively sacral powers of the community are the normative bearers of meaning and truth. The drives and possibilities of the self that are not related to these sacral powers tend to be ignored or repressed. On the other hand, when the latter situation does not merely reflect loss of confidence in certain traditional social structures and systems of symbols—and often today it means no more than this—but, instead, arises from faith in holy presence and power that may be encountered in all times and places, man is freed to explore every possibility latent in self and world. God is the ground of all that is, the supreme instance of actuality who liberates man, wherever he happens to stand, to contribute in his own distinctive finite fashion to the expansion of the realm of the actual.

The decisive instance of grace is bound up with the presence of God in Jesus Christ, then, in the further sense that it leads to a sort of appreciative secularity that permits the maximum realization of the potential inherent in self, community, and world. All the images and rituals of the Christian tradition are intended to orient the believer toward the *saeculum* and to afford him clues for the interpretation of the contemporary divine activity there. In this final sense, men find grace in nature—not only intimations and shadows of what they have received more fully within the church, but by means of the church resources to recognize that in the midst of nature they stand veritably in the presence of God. The diffusion of things that secularization denotes is the logical and, indeed, inevitable outcome of the Christian tradition. But it is a volatile affair. As the weirdness of contemporary quests for ecstasy attests, it may also pose the greatest challenge that Christianity has faced in two thousand years.

X

NATURE AND GRACE

"Nature and Grace" has been the most
persistent and one of the most important polarities employed in the history of systematic
Christian reflection. But if it has stubbornly en-
dured, it has been stubborn in other ways as
well. When the words have been used in some
disjunctive fashion, as though they represented
antagonistic principles, theology has seemed
more gnostic or Manichean than Christian.
Man has dwindled to half angel, half beast. On
the other hand, when the terms have been used
too hastily in a conjunctive way, as allies rather
than enemies, theology has sometimes appeared
more pagan than Christian. In either instance,
the polarity has too often been interpreted in
some quantifying fashion—as though it were ne-

cessary to separate and then paste back together again two different entities—that has done violence to the unity and dynamism of human existence. The various ways in which the polarity has been qualified by distinctions between common and saving, or prevenient and cooperating, grace have not really rendered it more useful for the interpretation of experience. Instead, they have simply borne their own testimony to its fundamental inadequacy and to man's irrepressible ingenuity. The polarity of "Nature and Grace" should be abandoned; it does not serve well as a significant principle of organization for Christian thought.

Grace is a useful word, for it designates the presence of the holy for and with men and underscores the fact that this presence is more than men can either expect or deserve. Second, it designates the triadic structure of community and acceptance and empowering without which the natural organism cannot achieve selfhood, but of which there are many and varied instances within this world. Therefore, it implies the essentially social and dependent nature of the self. Finally, it suggests that authentic existence involves being grateful, being graceful, and being gracious—three words now rather unfashionable, but perhaps no less important because of that. There are better arbiters of signifi-

139

cance than fashion.

But there is as much to be said against the idea of nature as there is in behalf of the concept of grace. It is the nature of man to transcend nature; any attempt to write of his nature can very quickly minimize the proportions of human liberty and creativeness, as well as the power of the imagination to project new possibilities for self-transcendence. Then, too, what is regarded as an instance of human nature by one generation may seem only an anachronism to the next. Reason is shaped by historical and cultural circumstances, and what seems universal one day may appear merely parochial very soon. In any event, it is *history* which is the real matrix and consequence of human life—a truth which reliance on the idea of nature can do nothing except obscure. Furthermore, it seems impossible to divest the theological notion of nature of its implicit reference to something else called supernature, about which the only certainty would seem to be that it is far away. This implication renders the polarity of "Nature and Grace" even less useful than it might otherwise be, for it masks the reality of grace in nature and distorts awareness of the many ways that grace is supplanted by mere similitudes of itself within the allegedly supranatural church.

140

Yet the inadequacy of the polarity stems from far more than the deficiencies involved in the idea of nature. Sometimes the distinction suffers from the same liabilities that flaw the polarities of religious and secular and of sacred and profane. On the one hand, there are so many instances of grace in nature. Indeed, if this were not true it is difficult to understand how one could recognize and respond to what Christians regard as the supreme instance of grace. On the other hand, there is so much of nature involved in grace, for better as well as for worse. In a sense, the intention of grace is simply the achievement of "nature"—that man might become more fully and deeply man. Furthermore, grace is mediated through the church by the same structures and operations by which it is mediated through other societies. Then, too, within the church as in other communities, grace is constantly reduced to various simulacra of itself. Sometimes, even when grace seems most truly grace, it may trap the believer, through his participation in this community, into relationships with other groups that are manifestly reactionary and socially disfunctional. But the principal objection to the polarity remains its static and quantifying character, for which there seems no cure. No matter how sensitive one may be to the dynamic interpenetra-

tion of the realities that nature and grace designate, the distinction still tends to isolate instead
of unite, fix instead of free, require a thousand
qualifications and perpetuate a great many
anachronous ideas. It is better to speak of the
holy and the human than of the sacred and
the profane or of the religious and the secular.
*Might it not be well to replace "Nature and Grace"
with a new polarity—the Everyday and Play?* Let us
sketch some reasons for the change.

Like all other intellectual ventures, theology
requires a *Denkform*. In other words, there must
be some *gestalt* or master image that informs
and organizes the whole, so that the relationships between its various parts are clear and
persuasive. Because theology deals with the
transition from inauthentic to authentic existence, which persons are enabled to undertake
only because of the presence of God for and
with man, this master image must be polar.
Because the theological enterprise is intended to
assist man in this transition, or at least not to
hinder him too much, the polarity must be sufficiently concrete to inspire human action. Within the Bible, there are various polarities, not
one; there are such juxtapositions as chaos and
cosmos, ignorance and knowledge, copy and
reality and slavery and freedom. In the history
of Christian thought, however, two have been

espccially important: "Law and Gospel" is one,
"Nature and Grace" the other. "The Everyday
and Play" has nothing to recommend it except
n ovelty unless it can state and relate more satisfactorily the motifs involved in these other polarities, *which themselves are not synonymous with the
distinction between inauthentic and authentic life.*
Neither nature nor law nor the everyday—after
all, who can do without the defenses of con-
vention and routine?—is unambiguously ranged
against the holy.

First of all, this polarity captures the actual
interplay of the authentic and inauthentic
more fully and more explicitly than the
others do; it expresses the real ambiguity of
the realm of the natural, both its goodness
and its distortion, as well as the ambiguities of the church. On the one hand, there is
always a play impulse at work in the sphere of
the everyday, bringing a measure of redemption
to the routinization of things; as Huizinga quite
properly comments, "the great archetypal activities of human society are all permeated with
play from the start."[23] On the other, the everyday world can manifest itself within the realm
of play, where there can certainly be undue
seriousness, unfair exclusiveness, or exaggerat-
ed competitiveness. The busyness and noisiness
and restriction of the range of reason that some-

times seem endemic to secularization can cha-
racterize various sorts of play as well. Then, too,
every instance of play is ephemeral; play constantly succumbs to the pressures of the everyday, for it is a fragile project that requires vigi-
lance to sustain. Nevertheless, the master image
of man as player does endure, always promis-
ing that the everyday world and the everyday
self can be transformed and redeemed. The implications of the polarity, therefore, are these: that
the everyday must be cherished and affirmed
because it always contains a playful element,
that it can be transformed by the autonomous
creativeness of man when he acts upon the
master image of the self that grace affords, and
that he must always be vigilant to discriminate
among various forms of play for these, like all
else within the world, have their ambiguities.

Second, the Everyday and Play expresses the
proper and genuinely internal relationship not
only of nature and grace but of law and Gospel
as well. Salvation is achieved when the play
impulse in the everyday finds free and complete
expression and controls the autonomous imagination—not when grace "elevates" nature
beyond itself, not when law is "swallowed up"
by Gospel. Playing offers men freedom by way
of order, an order that is freely embraced and
that does not violate the autonomy of the self.

144

To understand man as a player is not to fall into a new form of "works righteousness", wherein man seeks to justify himself by following the rules intrinsic to the game. Instead, it is the best possible antidote for the belief that man either can or need justify his ways and works. The perennially conflicting dionysian and apollonian impulses find their reconciliation. So the relation of order and liberty is phrased in more balanced and integral fashion than has often been achieved by reliance on the distinction between law and gospel. The Gospel calls man to play, but he cannot play apart from the law. Playing is a natural impulse that first appears in the everyday world of the law—a sign of man's freedom, a proleptic realization of what he is called to be, a witness to his relationship to that which transcends and judges all the principalities and powers of the market-place.

This polarity has far more contemporary relevance, perhaps, than do more traditional distinctions. No consequence of secularization is so baneful as the mood of self-seriousness that it breeds, especially because the most important implicate of revelation is a comic perception of life. Then, too, the putative loss of agency in the public realm that secularization implies is often reinforced by recourse to forms of "entertainment" in which the self is only a spectator and never really a participant. So even the private realm and prevailing uses of leisure time compound the sense of the loss of agency. Never has it been more urgent to recover the image of man as a player—to inhibit our seriousness, to restore our conviction of agency, to defend us from our passion for nothing except bread and circuses. The image invites man to join with the holy in the creation of new worlds, in new contributions to the increase of freedom and the enrichment of the realm of the actual.

As a normative category, playing does not suffer from some of the deficiencies of the idea of the natural, which is so empty of significant content that it is peculiarly susceptible to contingent and parochial accretions. It can perform all the prescriptive functions of the latter, while also placing greater emphasis on liberty and autonomy, creativeness and the power of self-transcendence. On the other hand, the idea of the everyday is able to give clear expression to the fact that sin includes, not least of all, transgressions against the self, as well as against the neighbor. Everydayness means the dissipation and loss of the self in subservience to the dictates of routine and public opinion, the repression of vital drives that conflict with common *mores*. It means gauging the worth of the self in material terms, or

146

the instrumental use of human beings, or the acceptance of the tyranny of "they say". The idea of the everyday is able to give proper weight to "the small sins" that often seem the very greatest of all—lack of involvement, thoughtlessness, insensitivity, habit and all the rest. It is, of course, as applicable to the church as to the world, and sometimes more so. Everydayness is a concrete and definite image; yet it is indefinitely capable of expansion as well.

When man is grasped by the holy, he finds himself in a comic universe and discovers his own liberties and responsibilities by way of the master image of the player. All men play sometimes, but the man who has been encountered by the holy is different because he is a grateful player. This gratitude finds its proper expression in creativeness and the highest form of creativity is the act of reconciliation. Grace means the presence of God for and with man. But God does not encounter man in isolation or leave him unchanged. So there are dimensions of grace: community, acceptence, and empowering or the enrichment of imagination. Upon these three depends the extent to which the promise of a fourth dimension of grace can be realized: the opportunity for creativeness. Man is made for this, not for captivity in old worlds but for the building of new ones—with the help of God.

147

NOTES

PART ONE

1. Herbert Braun, "The Problem of a New Testament Theology," in *Toward a New Christianity*, ed. Thomas J. Altizer (New York: Harcourt, Brace & World, 1967), p. 215.
2. Peter L. Berger, *A Rumor of Angels* (Garden City, N.Y.: Doubleday & Co., 1969), p. 68.
3. Thomas Luckmann, "Secularization—A Contemporary Myth" (lecture delivered at the University of Virginia, May 1969).
4. Peter L. Berger, *The Sacred Canopy* (Garden City, N.Y.: Doubleday & Co., 1967), p. 93.
5. John E. Smith, *Experience and God* (New York: Oxford University Press, 1968), p. 59.
6. Igor Stravinsky, *Poetics of Music in the Form of Six Lessons*, tr. Arthur Knodel and Ingolf Dahl (New York: Random House, Vintage Books, 1959), pp. 66-68.
7. Hans Urs von Balthasar, *Science, Religion and Christianity*, tr. Hilda Graef (London: Burns, Oates and Washbourne, 1958), pp. 142-43.
8. Martin Buber, *I and Thou*, tr. Ronald Gregor Smith (2d ed. New York: Charles Scribner's Sons, 1958), p. 3.
9. Albert Camus, *The Fall*, tr. Justin O'Brien (New York: Alfred A. Knopf, 1956), pp. 38-39.
10. Berger, *The Sacred Canopy*, p. 83.

11. Leo Tolstoy, *The Death of Ivan Ilych and Other Stories*, tr. Aylmer Maude and J. D. Duff (New York: New American Library, Signet Books, 1960), pp. 131-32.
12. T. S. Eliot, "Choruses from 'The Rock,'" from *Collected Poems, 1909-1962* (New York: Harcourt, Brace & World, 1963).
13. Smith, *op. cit.*, p. 66.
14. Erik Erikson, *Identity and the Life Cycle*, quoted in William F. Lynch, *Images of Hope* (New York: New American Library, Mentor Books, 1966), pp. 237, 240.
15. Julian N. Hartt, "Modern Images of Man," *Central Conference American Rabbis Journal* (June 1969), p. 17.
16. Julian N. Hartt, "Secularity and the Transcendence of God," in *Secularization and the Protestant Prospect*, ed. James F. Childress and David B. Harned (Philadelphia: Westminster Press, 1970), p. 158.
17. Wilfred Cantwell Smith, *The Meaning and End of Religion* (New York: New American Library, Mentor Books, 1964), p. 21.

PART TWO

1. John B. Cobb, *The Structure of Christian Existence* (Philadelphia: Westminster Press, 1967), p. 16.
2. *Ibid.*, p. 116.
3. *Ibid.*, p. 124.
4. Johan Huizinga, *Homo Ludens: A Study of the Play Element in Culture* (Boston: Beacon Press, 1955), p. 8.
5. *Ibid.*, p. 8.
6. *Ibid.*, p. 4.
7. *Ibid.*, p. 46.
8. Albert Camus, *The Rebel*, tr. Anthony Bower (New York: Random House, Vintage Books, 1954), p. 253.
9. Hartt, "Modern Images of Man," p. 12.
10. Stravinsky, *loc. cit.*
11. Huizinga, *op. cit.*, pp. 10-11.
12. Alan Paton, *Cry, The Beloved Country* (New York: Charles Scribner's Sons, 1950), p. 148.
13. *Ibid.*, p. 79.

14. Erich Fromm, *Man for Himself* (New York: Fawcett World Library, Premier Books, 1967), p. 81.
15. *Ibid.*, p. 95.
16. *Ibid.*, p. 97.
17. Nicolas Berdyaev, *Freedom and the Spirit*, tr. Oliver F. Clarke (London: Geoffrey Bles, 1935), pp. 209-10.
18. Nicolas Berdyaev, *The Destiny of Man*, tr. Natalie Duddington (New York: Harper & Bros., 1960), p. 144.
19. Karl Barth, *Dogmatics in Outline*, tr. G. T. Thomson (London: Student Christian Movement Press, 1949), p. 54.
20. Ignazio Silone, *Bread and Wine*, tr. Gwenda David and Eric Mosbacher (New York: New American Library, Signet Books, 1946), p. 248.
21. Reinhold Niebuhr, *Man's Nature and His Communities* (New York: Charles Scribner's Sons, 1965), p. 110.
22. *Ibid.*, p. 123.
23. Huizinga, *loc. cit.*